The Story of Louth
HOUSE OF CORRECTION
1671 - 1872

by
Bill Painter

Published by

Louth **N**aturalists', **A**ntiquarian and **L**iterary **S**ociety
The Museum, 4 Broadbank, Louth LN11 0EQ
Tel: 01507 601211
2004

©Bill Painter 2004

ISBN 0 9539533 2 7

To Alice

The right of Bill Painter to be identified as the author
of this work has been asserted by him in
accordance with the Copyright, Designs and
Patents Act 1988

All rights reserved. No part of this book may be reproduced, stored in a retrieval system, nor transmitted in any form nor by any means, electronic, mechanical, photocopying, whether recording or otherwise, without the prior permission in writing of the copyright holder or his authorised agent.

Contents

Foreword — 5

Chapter 1 – **Bridewell** — 7
The concept of the bridewell and the dissolute pauper. A simple justice system. The origins of the House of Correction in Louth.

Chapter 2 – **The Old Corporation** — 13
Alternative forms of punishment. The corporation, the justices and quarter sessions courts. The great fire at Barton-on-Humber. The early years. The story of John Keale – hanged at Haugham.

Chapter 3 – **To 'a land beyond the sea'** — 21
Minor offenders, rogues and vagabonds. Transportation. The ruinous state of the gaol.

Chapter 4 – **Sloth and Debauchery** — 29
John Howard and prison reform. Conditions within the county's common gaols and houses of correction. The tale of Rebecca Boulton – transported to Australia.

Chapter 5 – **Against the Peace** — 39
More inmates – greater squalor. A new bridewell at Kirton. Eleanor Coupland – whipped through the market place at Alford. Vagrancy. A day in court.

Chapter 6 – **A 'Working System'** — 51
Enlargement of the House of Correction and the fire of 1804. Segregation of a sort. John Stotherd's flight from custody. Conditions within. Further developments to become the busiest prison in the county.

Chapter 7 – **Hard Labour** — 63
The corn laws and agricultural unrest. Overcrowding. More troubles with 'casuals'. The first penitentiaries. Refurbishment and the treadwheel.

Chapter 8 – **New Eastgate Jail – old problems** — 77
A 'working system' overwhelmed. A new prison at Spilsby. The prison inspectors. Considerable room for improvement.

Chapter 9 – **Beyond Redemption** — 93
A new corporation. Belated attempts at reform. Education. The 'silent system'. Unsuitable accommodation. The county treasurer absconds. Closure.

Epilogue — 115

Appendix Report of the Reverend Isaac Russell, prison chaplain — 120

Sources and Bibliography — 123

Acknowledgments

It is fair to say a history of Louth House of Correction would not have been possible without the assistance and good humour of the principals and staff at Lincolnshire Archives Office. Access to their knowledge and understanding of the surviving Lindsey Quarter Sessions records was an essential aid in researching the life of the town's jail, and I am indebted to their assistance.

Catherine Fell, Librarian for the Prison Officers Training College at Newbold Revell, was helpful and enthusiastic. Not only did she make old prison records available to me, but afforded me an insight into modern practises.

The figures on the front cover and the turnkey facing page 7 are reproduced from articles dated 10th July 1852 and 22nd March 1873 by kind permission of the Illustrated London News Picture Library.

The painting of the Prison on the back cover is reproduced from William Brown's Panorama of Louth (1844-47), by kind permission of Louth Town Council.

My thanks to David Robinson for his suggestions on the text. His words of guidance and his patience whilst they took effect have proved invaluable.

My wife, Ann, has read the draft so many times, she probably knows more about Louth Prison than I do. She has taken a particular interest in the illustrations. Without her skills on the computer I would be lost. She has shown more dedication and enthusiasm than I deserve, and warrants a special mention.

Whilst acknowledging the role that others have played, responsibility for the final content remains mine.

Foreword

For the Victorians, prison was to be the 'central institution in the struggle against crime'. In the new model penitentiaries convicts would be broken and reformed. This Victorian regime had such a powerful impact that the names of the great prisons – Pentonville, Millbank, Dartmoor – still resonate, and it created an image, a hope of order and reformation, which still exerts a powerful influence today. It is, of course, a false image. It is false simply because most Victorian prisoners did not serve their time in the large government convict prisons. The overwhelming majority served a short sentence of a few days or weeks in a small local prison. We need to know more about these local gaols because it is there we find the reality of prison life in the past.

Bill Painter's book opens this reality. His history of 'Lincolnshire's busiest prison' takes us behind the headlines to reveal the difference between national policies and local hard facts. Lincolnshire conditions, pressures and personalities meant that in Louth things did not always work out as London intended.

The author not only gives us a thorough, detailed history, he has a good eye for personal experiences. His stories of those within the prison walls, told clearly and with humanity, offer glimpses of how the very poorest lived. There are some fascinating details too: the man with no toes, the grisly contents of the basket in Watch Tower passage, and 'Bleeding Old Nelly'.

This is a welcome sequel to Bill Painter's earlier study of the Workhouse. It makes a valuable contribution to the history of crime, but casts its net wide in social history and will be read with interest and enjoyment by all of us who would like to understand more of the history of our family, town or county in the eighteenth and nineteenth centuries.

Brian Davey
Keelby

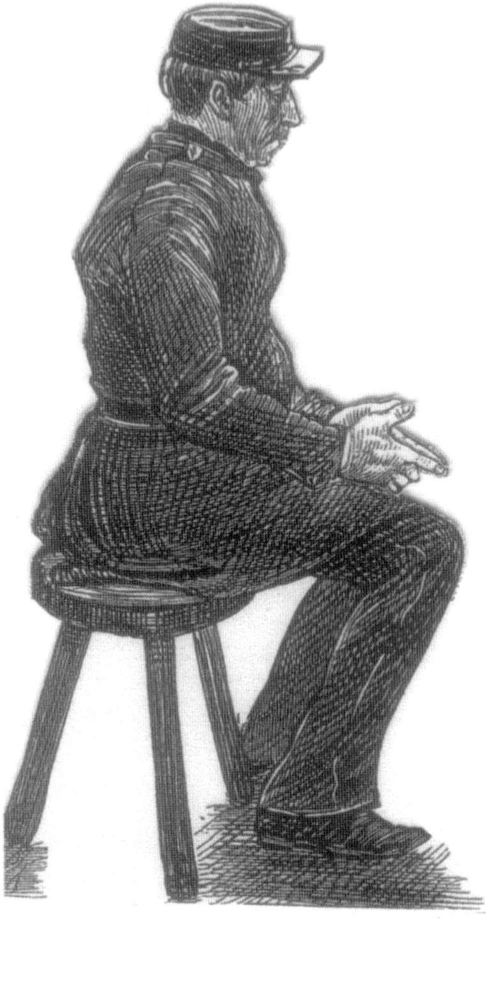

- 1 -

Bridewell

FOR many years the House of Correction at Louth was the busiest prison in Lincolnshire. Follow the main thoroughfare of Eastgate from the Market Place to the War Memorial, and the land where the Rev Frederick Orme's almshouses now stand, was the site of the town's gaol. A whipping post and tread wheels, 'dark' cells and shot drill, airing yards and hemp sheds once sullied these fair lawns.

The decision by the Grand Jury to close the gaol in 1872 met strong local opposition. The idea of Louth without a place of correction for rogues and vagabonds was unthinkable. It was surely central to the maintenance of law and order. Without fear of punishment, harlots, sturdy beggars and tricksters might seize the streets. Servants and labourers would be uncontrollable. Thieves could run free. To local tradesmen the running of the gaol required provisions, skills and services, and was a source of income. This place of punishment and retribution played an important role in the lives of local people. Overcrowded, unsanitary, and inadequate, closure was perhaps inevitable. In the light of events that occurred, relocation of the county gaol to Greetham, indeed anywhere apart from Louth, was understandable.

The story peels back the layers of time to help us understand the importance of a house of correction in a rural area. We glimpse the lives of the prisoners and witness their struggle to survive. We follow the workings of the local courts, and the hopeless task of the system in attempting to reform the unrepentant. Not all the inmates were sinners. The guilty sometimes ran free. The tale ends in corruption and betrayal.

When the prison was demolished Louth was the third largest town in Lincolnshire at the hub of a rich agricultural area known as East Lindsey. For more than 200 years the local justices of the peace had been committing the felons and misdemeanants of the region to the

House of Correction at Louth. The imposing entrance to the gaol was in Eastgate, (then known as Watery Lane). Behind the perimeter wall were two distinct buildings, the new prison and the old house of correction.

The new prison dated from 1826 when the justices sort yet again to extend and enlarge the capacity of the original buildings. The population of the town was increasing rapidly and there was considerable agricultural unrest. The numbers committed to prison at the local courts swamped the capacity of the old gaol. For those detained in the old prison, more usually referred to as the House of Correction, conditions were grim. Shared beds in a common ward, little segregation of the young from more hardened criminals. Vagrants and debtors thrown together and locked in the wards from dusk to dawn. No baths, kitchen, infirmary or reception rooms. The situation the inmates found themselves in of little concern to the people of the town. Nominally under the supervision of Lindsey justices and financed by a local rate the town gaol was probably looked upon as an extension of the already too generous assistance given the poor. The prisoners only had themselves to blame for their predicament. There were more important matters to resolve.

A more enlightened approach to the treatment of prison inmates had been urged by the reformer John Howard some 40 years earlier. But in the 1780's the country was recovering from the American war of independence and contemplating conflict with Napoleon's France. There was much talk of reform, but little action. Members of the town Corporation, an unelected body, oversaw the piecemeal development of this sad and lonely habitation in Ramsgate. In 1750 it was barely sufficient for the safe keeping of the inmates, the justices finding the House of Correction to be in such a ruinous and dilapidated condition that the dwelling house of the keeper was liable to fall down.

The first houses of correction had been established under the Elizabethan Poor Laws. In Tudor times one of the Royal Palaces near St. Bride's well on the Thames fell into decay. Following on its use as an infirmary, it was adapted to house and occupy the destitute poor. When an Act of 1609 required idle rogues and vagabonds to be set to work to mend them of their indolent ways, the institutions they were sent to were modelled upon the former palace. These houses of correction became known as bridewells. They provided an alternative to houses of industry in towns and poor houses in the village intended for the impotent poor - paupers reduced to destitution through no fault of their own. Bridewells and the houses of correction were intended to coerce vagrants and dissolute paupers, petty offenders and idle apprentices into a more industrious life. They were not the responsibility of central government but of the local administration. In exchange for productive work the inmates were supplied their food and keep.

Haberdashers, Hosiers, Hatters
The prisoners made up calico, worsted, cotton, hessian and linen purchased from local traders, into dresses, trousers and shirts, blankets and bed rugs.
Lindsey Quarters Sessions A/1/622/21
Lincolnshire Archives office

Edward VI's charter established Louth's corporation of a Warden and six Assistants, but not until 1607, under James I, were the same men given municipal authority to govern the town and raise taxes to pay their charges. Assistants in Louth were appointed for life, and the post of Warden normally taken in turn. They chose their own successors. Members of the corporation were the towns' ruling elite. They appointed the High Steward, a Town Clerk, a Treasurer for the county funds, a bailiff to enforce their byelaws, and the chief constables. The Warden and one of his Assistants were sworn as justices of the peace and formed the judiciary. They experienced little difficulty in maintaining their authority. The system was far from democratic, but the justices were answerable for their decisions and quickly recognised in the town. The courts remained the only way in which aggrieved parties might seek justice. The jury were quite ready to dismiss those cases they found wanting, and this went some way towards instilling confidence in the system. Local courts were known as petty and quarter sessions, and tried all matters brought before them except treason, felony and murder.

This was a time when imprisonment was not used as a form of correction but to ensure offenders were brought to justice. The punishment of offenders was simple, physical and often brutal. For

Petty Jurors and a public whipping
The King against Mary Wright. Convicted of petty theft by the jury of 12 men, she received the usual punishment. A public whipping through the market place considered a good example to others. 1731 marked the end of the use of Latin in Corporation Records.
Louth UDC Sessions Record 1721-1742
Lincolnshire Archives Office

committing public nuisance and misdemeanours, ne'er-do-wells were placed in the town stocks. The accounts of the Old Corporation record that in 1610, Long, the smithy, repaired the irons for the stocks, and in 1637 the frame of the pillory was replaced. Vagrants and beggars might be burned in the hand, whilst persistent reprobates suffered a public whipping. Mawborne supplied bolts and irons (manacles and shackles) for the whipping post in 1641, and William Gunis was paid six shillings (30p) for similar work 25 years later. Most felonies (including theft of property worth more than a shilling [5pence]) were capital offences dealt with at the County Assize. Hanging or transportation awaited the convict.

At the beginning of the 17th century the county of Lincolnshire was an isolated and thinly populated land. Poor communications in the county were made worse by the lack of bridges over the Trent and Witham, and the difficulty of travel around the Wash. The county was divided into three parts, Holland, Kesteven and Lindsey. Lindsey was sub-divided again into east and west.

The Parts of Lindsey extended from the River Witham in the south to the Humber in the north, and the Isle of Axholme and the River Trent in the west to the German Ocean (the North Sea). Agriculture and sheep supported a number of small market towns. In Lindsey there were regular courts of quarter session at Spittal, Caistor, Louth, Horncastle, Spilsby, Gainsborough, Kirton and Lincoln. The magistrates convened elsewhere according to need. The castle prison at Lincoln was used for debtors and for those awaiting trial at the assize, transportation or execution. The lock-up in the Stonebow Gate housed the city prisoners. Justices of the peace were to provide local houses of correction or bridewells for resolving the problem of vagrancy, and they, and the common gaols, could be used to detain persons awaiting trial or punishment. The county prisons for East Lindsey were located in Gainsborough and Louth where it was known as the House of Correction.

Louth was little affected by the Civil War, but in 1631, following an outbreak of the plague, 725 townspeople died. It seems likely half the inhabitants lost their lives. The market was suspended and food left for the people a mile south of town at the 'Saturday Pits'.

Louth House of Correction is first mentioned in 1671.

Warden and his Assistant
Lindsey Quarter Sessions A/1/280/37
Lincolnshire Archives Office

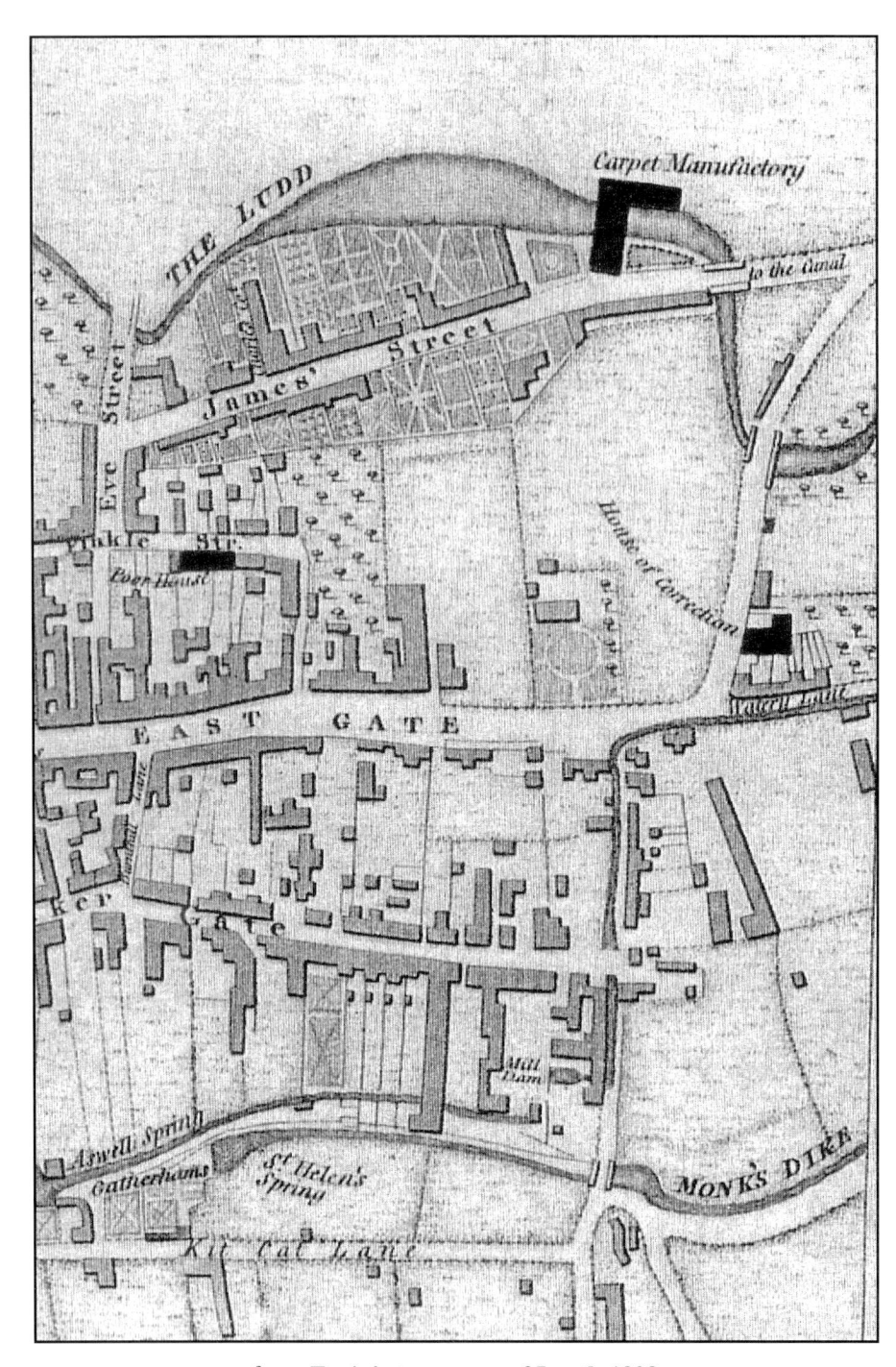

from **Espin's town map of Louth 1808**
Three corporate buildings: the Poor House for the paupers; the Carpet Manufactory as a place to labour; the House of Correction for the mendicant.
Lincolnshire Local Studies Library

- 2 -

The Old Corporation

THE records of the Old Corporation show Louth to be well equipped to discipline troublesome citizens. The town stocks were certainly in place till 1650, possibly in the Fish Shambles, where two stocks allowed more than one person at a time to be publicly ridiculed. The pillory was in the Market Place, similar to the stocks, but the wrongdoer stood with wrists and neck, thrust through holes in two planks of wood fixed to a post or wooden framework. The pillory was a more substantial structure than the stocks, with painted iron and timberwork, and a roof tiled against the weather. The ducking stool mentioned in the records was probably near Faulkner's Mill where the new bridge crossed the River Lud. The whipping post near the town hall was a very public warning of the likely fate for wrongdoers brought before the magistrates.

Most law enforcement was the result of prosecution by private individuals, though petty or parish constables, churchwardens and overseers of the poor helped with proceedings in their own fields. Whilst detection and arrest was difficult, punishment followed swiftly upon conviction and was often public and painful.

Courts were held before the Justices of the Peace in the tiny Sessions Hall, in the southwest corner of the Market Place. The hall was mounted on chamfered pillars above the butter cross. On market days ten local women sold butter in the open space beneath on payment of a penny a stall. Access to the courtroom was by means of a flight of stone steps to the first floor, where the Royal coat of arms was painted above the doorway. Inside were a long table, and chairs for the Bench and the Clerk. Members of the jury, and everyone else, were expected to stand. To one side a cage or dungeon secured prisoners of the court. Corporation accounts show that in 1606 they incurred expenses for *mendinge the Cage lock when the hall Dore was broken by a roagge who escaped away.* The roof space or garret was sufficiently large to be used as a rather ill lit jury room. Being above ground level, the hall was difficult to maintain, and by 1714 it was *so very much decayed and out of repairs* the Corporation were obliged to remove the old thatched roof and build another topped with a fine bell and clock tower with four painted dial plates.

Coat of Arms
Many forms used by the justices were pre printed. George II's coat of arms above, heads a settlement examination before the court in the 1730s
Lindsey Quarter Sessions A/1/51/9
Lincolnshire Archives Office

Local courts were not only concerned with the prosecution of offenders. The link between the justices of Louth and the town corporation ensured some of their time was spent on the administration of the borough. The courts fixed the price of bread and salt and beer, and oversaw the alehouses. Appearances in court for tippling or drawing ale without a licence were numerous, and closely associated with the keeping of bawdy houses where the proprietor was often a woman. In 1734, Ann Dixon was brought before the court by the officers of Horncastle for keeping a lewd and disorderly house. The court ordered the *Sign of the said Ann Dixon be pulled Down and she be putt Down for Brewing and her surety Estreated*. Clearly unlawful games had been sanctioned in her victualling house.

Orders were issued for the highways to be repaired and the streets cleaned. John Clarke was appointed town scavenger to clean the pavements and remove the dirt from the back streets. Dissenters from the Church of England likely to hold public office (including members of the Cracroft, Massingberd and Wrigglesworth families, sometime Wardens of Louth) took an oath of allegiance to the Crown and renounced popery. Preaching houses were allowed for Quakers, Presbyterians and Independants. The courts regulated street markets and monitored the price, weight and quality of traded goods including salt, bread and spirituous liquors. This sometimes gave rise to anomalies as when the price of wheat rose and fell, the 'weight' of a seven pound loaf might vary. For the prisoners in the House of Correction allowed two penny loaves a day at eight ounces each, this often meant less food. Joseph Payne exposed bad beef for sale. Thomas Walker of Thorpe was found *weighing wool with a Bad Weight which he pretended to be half a stone when in fact it was only six pounds*, and Charles Codogan and John Sergeant bought butter at Brigg market to sell at Caistor for a profit. Regarded now perhaps as good business practice, but then considered 'engrossment'. Gamekeepers were licensed and woolwinders affirmed as to their honesty.

The great fire that broke out around the market place in Barton on Humber in the early hours of Friday 11th December 1730 destroyed 48 bays of buildings. Before the introduction of clay pantile roofs, thatch of straw and reed was a significant fire hazard in any town. There were no fatalities, but the homes of eight families were destroyed, the flames consumed the greatest part of their household goods, working tools and utensils and implements of husbandry. The sufferers and their families narrowly escaped with their lives. It was to the court of quarter sessions at Louth that application was made under the Great Seal of Great Britain for charitable relief by the benevolence of well-disposed persons in the county.

There were disputes to settle and delicate matters to resolve. In a time when the cost of the poor was born by the parish, the arrival of travellers in a village was a cause for concern. A man unable to find sufficient work to support his family became a charge upon the local rate. Churchwardens and overseers of the poor were quick to apply to a justice of the peace for an order removing the stranger, his wife and children to their last legal place of settlement. In the meantime they were detained in the House of Correction. Removals disputed by the receiving parish might prove expensive, especially if legal advice was obtained. Such action was not lightly undertaken.

Similarly, children of unmarried women might also constitute a financial expense. When a single woman was known to be pregnant she was brought before the magistrate and examined as to the identity of the man responsible. He, together with his own father as surety, was bound over to appear before the court. As the putative parent he was expected to bear the costs of the mother's lying in, her nursing care and other charges associated with having the baby, the costs of the court, and the maintenance until at least eight years old when the child might enter service. Charges might be considerable, but if he demurred the probability of a stay in the House of Correction often helped make up his mind. Forced recruitment into his Majesty's sea or land services was deemed nearly as unpleasant as detention in the gaol, and the two were often combined. Most accepted the judgement of the court in the hope it would not be for too long. At a time when only a third of all births survived to the age of five, the likelihood of a child of an unmarried mother reaching its first birthday were slim. Settlement disputes and bastardy orders absorbed a significant part of the justices' time.

In 1725 William Clarke was bound over to appear at the sessions for a breach of good behaviour committed against Joseph Chamberlain. Chamberlain was a justice of the peace, an Assistant of the Corporation and an extremely powerful man. Clarke was charged with affronting him in the execution of his office by refusing when required *to putt of his Hatt and saying he did not putt of his Hatt to such Scrubbs as he.*

Clarke surrendered to his recognisance, but was discharged when Chamberlain did not appear to prosecute his case. Perhaps sometimes the judgement of those in authority lacked confidence and wisdom.

Two magistrates sat at the weekly petty sessions dealing mainly with misdemeanours. They were often called upon to work from their own homes, taking written statements from witnesses, issuing arrest warrants and examining offenders. Their records, if there were any, have not survived.

At the quarter sessions two justices sitting with a jury of 12 men decided more serious matters. The parish constables prepared the jury list of parishioners and warned them to attend the court. If a juryman failed to appear, both he and the constable warning him were liable to a 20 shilling (£1) fine. A panel of 36 jurors was raised from five or six parishes. They were to be freemen owning or occupying their own property – the 'forty shilling freeholders'. There were two juries at each session. The Grand Jury, never less than 12 men, decided whether the evidence supported the charge and created a case to be answered. 'No Bill' meant the discharge of the prisoner after he paid the gaoler's fees. If the Grand Jury decided there was a 'True Bill' the matter was tried before the 12 men of the Petty jury. The jury was quite ready to dismiss those cases they found wanting, and this went some way towards instilling confidence in their decisions. Four justices sat at the trial of a felon, including either the Warden or his deputy.

The courts in Lindsey worked together and sat in rotation. Gainsborough and Spittal were the busiest, but Spilsby, Louth and Caistor were also centres of justice and met regularly. As the name suggests, quarter sessions met four times a year in the spring, summer, autumn and winter, when they were variously referred to as the Lent or Easter, Midsummer or Thomas a'Becket, Michaelmas, Christmas and Epiphany sessions. Minutes for the quarter sessions were recorded in

Thomas Green's confession
Written examination of the accused seldom gave reasons for the crime.
Lindsey Quarter Sessions Records A/27/7
Lincolnshire Archives Office

a ledger common to all and passed around the county. Local constables took prisoners ordered by the courts to be detained to the House of Correction at Gainsborough or Louth. The justices of the peace at the various courts were known to one another, and a 'grand jury', including justices from Kesteven and Holland, was responsible for the administration of the prison and the County Assize at Lincoln Castle.

Little is known of Louth House of Correction in the early years. We have no reason to believe the location of the House, in Ramsgate at the corner with Watery Lane, changed during its lifetime. Whilst referred to regularly as a place of detention in the surviving records of the quarter sessions, links with the poor law continued, and food, medical care and clothing were provided for the homeless in the prison. Ultimately responsible for the treatment of the inmates and the conditions in the house, the justices seldom thought it necessary to visit the site and report on their findings.

In keeping with other dwellings in the town, the House almost certainly comprised a mud and stud hovel thatched with straw. Sleeping and working rooms were communal. The windows provided for ventilation as much as for light, either barred or shuttered. Straw and sawdust covered the earth floors. It was secured at night by the keeper who provided a dietary of potatoes, meal and a little meat for the inmates to cook on an open fire. The House, work and exercise yard was surrounded by a stockade of spiked wooden palings. Perhaps pigs and geese were kept by the gaoler and his wife on land near by. Water from the springs at Ashwell ran into Watery Lane, past the prison across marshy ground, and into the River Lud. The House was not extensive and the few inmates awaited their fate at the next quarter sessions.

In 1671, Charles Kilborne, later the master, was keeping the house for his brother, and setting those committed to him to work and give them correction. The provision of some form of labour, productive or otherwise, was a constant problem for the keeper of the House, and one that was often ignored. Apart from the discipline needed to keep the inmates at work, the master was faced with problems of mixed abilities, age and sex, the likely poor physical condition of many of his charges, and the varying lengths of detention. The most common option was the purchase of hemp or flax to keep the prisoners at labour. The work was dirty, smelly and exhausting. The raw materials needed to be beaten and crushed with blocks and hammers, and left to foment, then beaten and crushed again. This continued action loosened the fibres allowing them to be spun on foot-driven mills and looms into coarse thread or whipcord that could be sold to rope makers in the town.

Louth was not merely a repository for local prisoners, but also for those committed to gaol by other courts in Lindsey. In 1699 the constables of Horncastle brought a woman of lewd life to the House at Louth on the instruction of the local magistrate. Louth in turn transferred some of its own prisoners to the castle at Lincoln. The justices reasoned that as they were obliged to contribute towards the gaol's costs, they intended to make use of it. Those sentenced to transportation to a land beyond the sea, the Americas and the West Indies, were dispatched and detained in the castle as a matter of course, but others liable to removal included violent or troublesome prisoners, those who had attempted to escape, and the debtors – a significant proportion of the prison population.

Debtors were intended to receive different treatment to other offenders to enable them to clear their account. Allowed tools of their trade, open access to their family, and additional food and drink, their presence in the smaller gaols where they were not segregated from other prisoners caused serious disciplinary problems. In reality they were treated the same as the other inmates. At the Easter sessions in Spilsby in 1706, the justices ordered that *five prisoners in the Castle at Lincoln for debt be delivered over to her Majesties Service at Sea unless they be discharged from their Creditors by May Day next, the officer that takes them to give the gaoler a receipt and pay him ten shillings (50p) for each man.* They were to be handed over to Capt. Henry Knight to serve in Colonel Charles Will's Regiment of Marines. Others were sent to serve as foot soldiers. Such orders by the court encouraged compliance with their directions, and helped keep the prisons empty.

It is unlikely that John Keale was detained for long in the House of Correction at Louth. Born about 1680 at Bardney Dairies where his parents had a smallholding, he squandered away his inheritance and drifted into service. He seemed both idle and extravagant. He was fortunate in meeting and marrying a young girl with money of her own, and they rented a small farm at Muckton, three miles from Louth. A contemporary pamphlet on the *Tryal of John Keale* describes his *wife proving a slattern at home and he a loyterer in the field, and taking more care to propagate children than to maintain them, he in a few years reduced himself, his wife and five children to poverty.* The family were reduced to pauperism *over-run with filth*. In 1723, after 15 years of marriage, his wife Elizabeth died.

Keale found occasional work as a labourer in Burwell, the next parish, and was fortunate in prevailing upon a local maidservant, Mary Aldgate, to be his second wife. Though much younger than Keale, she proved a careful and industrious women, and brought him three more children, two boys and a girl. The family did not prosper, and it seems that Keale's idleness and liking for strong drink soured Mary's feelings and may have led her to seek consolation elsewhere. John Keale became aware of his wife's *change of affection for a neighbour of whom he had lately entertained a hot suspicion, fancying in the youngest child he see his picture*.

One morning in early September 1730, the discontent in this wretched family spilled over, and in a fit of rage and jealousy, Keale snatched the innocent child, and despite his wife's struggles *with a furzebill chopt off its head on the edge of the cradle*. As his wife ran from the dwelling he struck her down the back between the shoulders, and caught her as she tried to climb the stile. Pulling her backwards he stabbed her in the chest and throat, killing her immediately.

Neighbours alerted by the cries detained Keale and he was brought before the magistrate at Louth. Justice Atkinson committed him to the castle at Lincoln to await his trial. The tragic event is recorded in Muckton parish register - *Mary the wife of John Keal and William his son both barbarously murthered (by) the said John Keal buried September 10th*.

Capital punishment could only be imposed at the County Assize. A judge called twice a year on a circuit from London. As well as murder and manslaughter, the death penalty applied to many offences including sedition (speaking against the king), all serious assaults, uttering bad money, and theft where violence was used or where the value of the property exceeded one shilling (5p). By 1800 more than two hundred transgressions were punishable by hanging. Local courts ensured most thefts were dealt with at quarter sessions by adjusting the 'value' of goods stolen to 10pence (4p) or less.

In the castle prison Keale was placed in heavy irons, and chained to the floor to await his trial. Six months later, on Tuesday 7th March 1731 at the Lent Assize in County Hall, he pleaded 'not guilty' to the murder of his wife and child. After hearing the evidence the jury convicted him. Lord Baron Page, the judge, remarked upon the barbarity of the act and Keale's lack of remorse. He was condemned to be gibbeted alive.

This was not a penalty allowed in law. After hanging, the bodies of convicted murderers were normally used for dissection and medical research. Those to be gibbeted as an example to others were covered in tar after death to slow down the process of decomposition. The body was then hung in chains or an iron cage from a gibbet at the roadside near the scene of their crime, *as a lasting monitor to all passengers to beware of these heinous and fatal crimes which had brought this poor wicked and bloodthirsty wretch to such a terrible and untimely end.*

From a pamphlet published at the time we learn that on the morning of Saturday 18th March 1731, John Keale, and the gibbet irons, were taken from Lincoln in a light cart, or tumbril, to Haugham Walk near the crossroads between Muckton, Burwell and Louth. He was hanged from the gibbet-post until he was dead, cut down, covered in tar, replaced in irons, and hung up again, *food for every devouring bird of prey*. The iron gibbet cage is now in Louth Museum. The entry in Muckton parish register continues - *The said John Keal was hanged in chains in Louth broad Spot March 18th.*

In 1798 two of the town's justices, Charles Massingberd and Marmaduke Alington agreed to a request that Haugham Walk, leading from Haugham to the turnpike between Louth and Spilsby, was no longer necessary and be stopped up. It no longer exists.

- 3 -

To 'a land beyond the sea'

FEAR of committal to the House of Correction empowered the authority of the county's magistrates. The presence of this shabby habitation just outside the town was as important as the parish constable in maintaining law and order. Given scant attention by those responsible for its operation, the years of neglect would eventually need to be paid for. The gaols at Gainsborough and Louth were used by the courts of Lindsey as repositories for those unable to care for themselves, the casuals 'on the tramp', petty thieves awaiting punishment, and debtors. Their days were spent in idleness.

In 1733 one of the prisoners, Jonathon Parrott, escaped from the House of Correction in Louth. As a result the keeper, William Maugham, was brought before the court, fined £5 and discharged from his office by the justices. No attempt appears to have been taken to improve security at the gaol, though repair and rebuilding work did take place at Gainsborough following a visit by the court. Maugham was replaced by George Rawson as keeper.

From Howgrave's *Stamford Mercury*, 20th March 1734: *Whereas the House of Correction in Louth, Lincolnshire, was lately broke by Thomas SCRIVIN of Barrow and John JOHNSON of Mareham in the Fenn, whereby they made their Escape; Thomas SCRIVIN is a very low Man, in grey Cloaths, and has brown Hair, 24 years of Age, of a fresh Compexion and wanting two Teeth before. John JOHNSON is a low Man of a black Complexion and black, thin, lank Hair, was in brown Cloaths when he made his Escape, and is very round Shoulder'd, having a Wife and Family in Mareham aforesaid.*
Whoever apprehends both, or either of the Persons above described, or gives Notice to George RAWSON of Louth so that they may be secured, shall be well Rewarded for their Trouble by me,
(signed) George RAWSON

George Rawson, the gaoler, will shortly be fined and replaced. Whilst conditions within the gaol were of little concern to the justices, the court was quite willing to use the House of Correction for their own ends. George Atterby, a grazier of Theddlethorpe, was produced by the keeper before a court sitting at Caistor in January 1766. Atterby had slandered and abused William Marshall, a member of the corporation and a justice of the peace, in Louth the previous market day. Having repeated his claims in court, and refused to withdraw his words, one hopes he was not surprised when he was returned to the House of Correction. He was to remain there for a month to contemplate his folly. On completion of the sentence he was required to provide security himself of £40 - a staggering sum - and two other sufficient sureties of £20 each for his good behaviour towards William Marshall in future.

Offenders against the public purse were also rigorously pursued. The management of the common lands was a particularly contentious matter and frequent overstocking resulted in a shortage of grazing. Fences surrounding the common were broken down and the stock driven onto adjacent cornfields and cow pastures owned by local farmers. Beasts, swine, sheep and geese found trespassing on enclosed lands were removed by the pinder to the parish pound. Julian Ballit and William Wharfe broke down the fences of the pound in the Poor Close, released their three geldings and drove them away *to the great damage of all liege subjects, and the Evil example of all others in the like Case offending and against the peace.* The magistrates viewed this as an all too common occurrence! They were both fined £10 and committed to the House of Correction till it was paid.

The least likely offences to result in detention were breaches of the peace and cases of assault. When Nicholas Dowd was brought before the magistrates for cursing and swearing several times in the public and open streets of Louth, or Elizabeth Bezel appeared at court for telling fortunes, they might reasonably expect to be bound over to be of good behaviour and find suitable sureties for there future conduct. This was not always the case. Simon Dales of Saleby was detained at Louth *upon the Oath of Sarah Dales* (his wife) … *that he had threatened to be the Death of her, and that she is afraid that he will wound or kill her or do her some bodily harm,* he was returned by the justices to the House of Correction until he found sufficient sureties to keep the peace especially towards his wife. Prisoners unable to raise their securities often remained in the House of Correction a considerable length of time.

The most likely persons to be detained in the House and set to hard labour were those described as casuals and vagrants. We do not know to what extent their number included the travelling poor. Those with previous convictions were dealt with as 'rogues and vagabonds' and might additionally expect to be publicly whipped in the market place. Husbands and wives travelling with children were detained at hard labour for seven days in the communal rooms of the House. The family was then returned to their last place of settlement by the constables on a warrant or pass.

Theft was the most likely felony to be dealt with by the court. Parishioners stole ducks and geese and conies, pieces of leather, woollen stockings, shifts and breeches, and treacle and wine from vessels stranded on the seashore. James Cook split a tree and carried away honey and wax. For stealing milk, Leonard Bycroft was detained in the House of Correction till market day when he was given 30 lashes in the Market Place at 12 noon. Most convicted thieves faced a public whipping.

Henry Raithby, a labourer from Tathwell, was brought before the quarter sessions at Louth in March 1733. He was charged with stealing two pecks of wheat (about a sack full). James Gostelow, the owner, valued the goods at two shillings (10p). The grand jury considered the facts of the case and decided there was a 'True Bill' to answer. Henry Raithby pleaded guilty. The court ordered his transportation, the most serious punishment that local justices were able to impose. Its seemingly arbitrary use was a most terrible penalty. Those brought before the local courts had seldom stolen anything of great value, yet their actions might provoke a devastating retribution.

Transportation
"Ordered that Sarah the Wife of William Royl and Bridget the wife of John Birth be transported into some of his Majesty's Dominions beyond the seas for seven years being found guilty of Two judicmts for Petty Larceny in Stealing Linen from Mr John Rowton and from Mr Thos Thorold".
Women only had an identity through their husbands and fathers.
Quarter Sessions record 1721-1742 Louth
Lincolnshire Archives Office

Transportation, 'to a land beyond the sea', was seldom for less than a term of seven years, and for many was a sentence of death. Those transported were most unlikely to see their families again. Following sentence, the convict was transferred to the castle prison at Lincoln. The keeper of the county gaol was responsible for their enshipment, and allowed eight guineas a-piece, plus expenses, recoverable from the county purse, for his trouble. When arrangements were complete the convicts were taken in chains to Blackwall or Woolwich docks in London to board the vessel. Shipped by the merchants of the slave trade to the West Indies or the American colonies of Virginia or the Carolinas, their labour was sold at the dockside to the highest bidder. Viewed as likely troublemakers, they fetched less than black slaves, who were better able to stand the heat, and their prospects were probably worse. They were not welcome migrants and resistance to their shipment steadily grew.

Accounts presented by the keeper of Lincoln prison indicate between five and fifteen men and women a year were sentenced to transportation by the courts of the county at the beginning of the 18th century.

The arrival of the turnpikes in the county and the completion of the canal – the Louth Navigation - improved communications and proved a bonus to commerce and industry. The population of the town and the surrounding parishes that had grown slowly in the first half of the century now began to increase more rapidly. The workload on the courts in Lindsey became such that business was seldom complete within the day. Rather than return for a second day in the courthouse, the justices regularly chose to complete their lists in a local hostelry. In Louth they adjourned to the *Blue Stone Inn* or the *Kings Head*, at Lincoln they chose the *Angel above Hill*, the *George* and the *White Hart* at Spilsby.

Locally these adjournments often preceded a larger social event, as when the constables were sworn. A session's dinner and entertainment, followed by tobacco and clay pipes, a bottle of wine for a preacher and a toast to the King's health, time for gossip, the exchange of scandal, and the furtherance of business interests.

A committee was formed to visit and inspect the House of Correction at Louth. They found the keeper's dwelling house and the prison in a ruinous state and very much out of repair. The day room, the only room with a fireplace, needed reinforcing with oak planking and ironwork. Perhaps there had been another escape.

When Rawson was discharged, John Marsden was appointed in his place. One of the bills he presented to the court provides us with an idea of the likely inmates: *for maintaining Mary Langley and her three Children, she being disordered in Mind the last Sessions and incapable of being examined to her Settlement.* £5 3s 8d (£5 18p).

By summer 1754 the keeper's house had fallen down and the Corporation were forced to accept the House of Correction was not sufficient for the safe keeping of prisoners. They authorised alterations

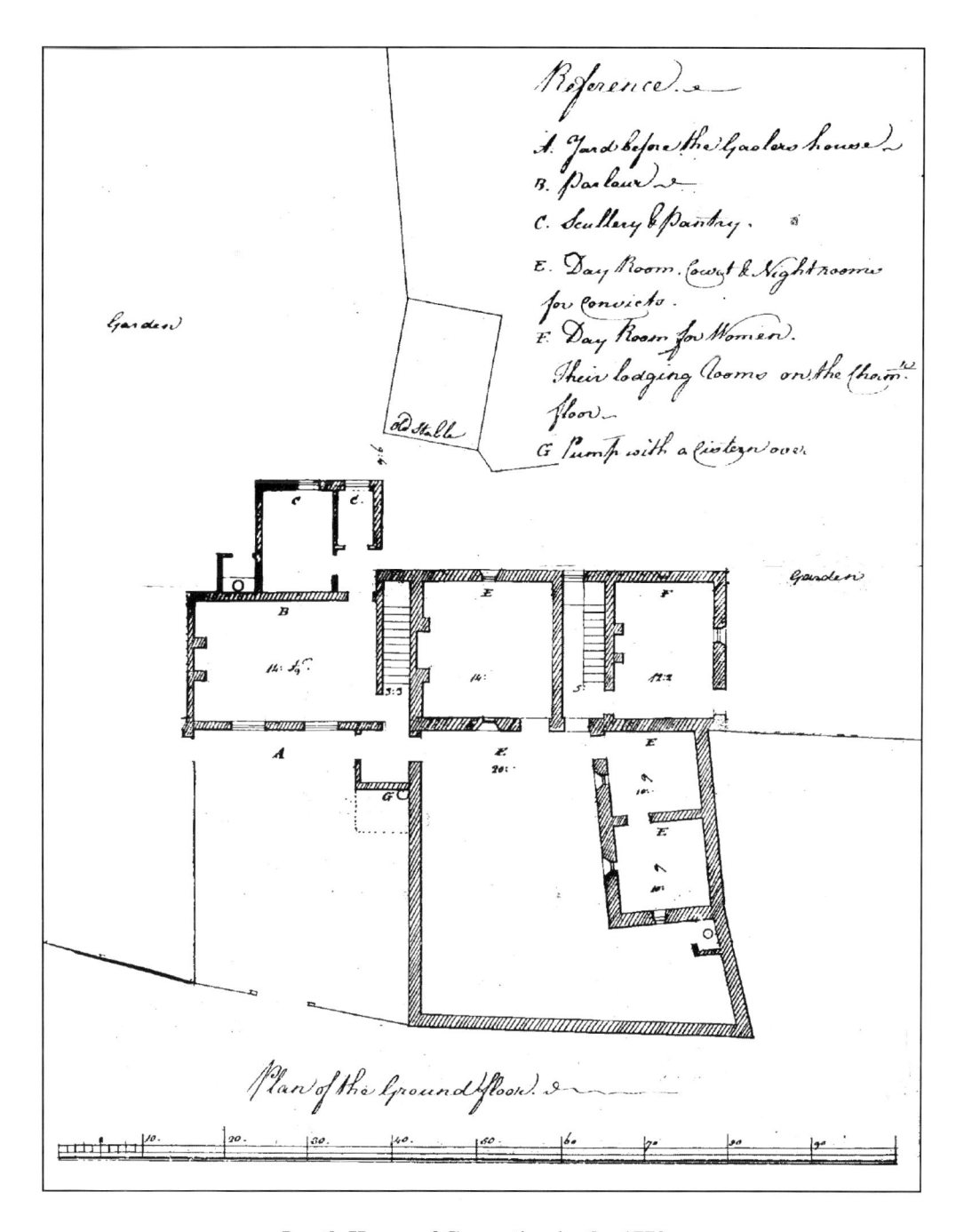

Louth House of Correction in the 1770s
The keeper's house on the left facing into Ramsgate. The sick were cared for in the room above the women's day room. Females slept in night chambers above the men overlooking the exercise court
**Lindsey Quarter Sessions. B/5/Louth 1786 No 1
Lincolnshire Archives Office**

and repairs and raised the outer fence. Charges were not to exceed £75. Two of the justices, David Atkinson and Robert Cracroft, were made responsible for the work and advised it was to be undertaken in a most frugal manner. Any savings they were able to make were to be returned to the county treasurer.

The opportunity was taken to replace the old dwelling of mud and stud with a new structure, as was happening elsewhere in the town at that time. Building on the same site in Ramsgate, not far to the south of the River Lud, the new prison of brick and tile included a lodging house for the keeper and separate sleeping wards for men and women. A further increase in expenditure made room for up to 20 prisoners, and the justices took the opportunity of reminding the chief and petty constables of the steady increase in those wandering abroad and not giving a good account of themselves. They were to be brought before the justices of the peace, examined and dealt with according to the law.

If the benefits of the turnpikes arriving in the south of the county were to be fully realised the local roads needed to be improved. Many rate payers needed encouragement. In 1757 the parishioners of Stewton were summoned before the quarter sessions when William Marshall, town Warden, found Louth House Lane between Manby and Tathwell *used for all the liege subjects of our Lord the King and his Predecessors with their Horses, Coaches, Carts and Carriages to go, return, pass, ride and labour at their Will ... was very ruinous, miry, deep broken and in such decay for want of Reparation and Amendment that the Liege subjects of the King could not use the carriageway without great danger to their lives and loss or great damage to their goods and Common Nuisance to the subjects , against the Peace of our Lord the King, his Crown and Dignity.* If the village was to avoid a fine, prompt repairs were needed.

Such industry provided opportunities for others. In 1764, Thomas Smith and his son dug up 40 feet of the roadway between Louth and Legbourne, and stole the sand and gravel so carefully laid. The Dexthorpe turnpike from Spilsby to Bawtry was the first to reach Louth in 1765.

As the highways improved, the justices realised the carriage of goods might also be controlled. Carters were allowed to charge four pence a stone in weight for every 20 miles covered, about the distance to Hull, Lincoln and Boston. When the military were in the area, the army were charged rather more. To carry their heavy equipment on day marches, they needed four wheeled wagons each drawn by six oxen, and charged at four pence a mile.

The Louth Navigation arrived at the Riverhead in 1770, connecting the town to the ports of Hull, Gainsborough, Boston and beyond. The export of grain and wool balanced the arrivals of cargoes of coal, timber and coggles of fish. Commercial development to the east of the House of Correction began.

By now the prison, a two storey brick and tile building within a perimeter wall, was more suited to the demands placed on it by the sentencing justices. Two work or day rooms gave onto an airing yard or exercise court with an open privy. The floor of the men's day room was paved, and a stout post set in the middle was fastened at the top to the joists of the floor above. The visiting justices directed that four chains be provided to secure the prisoners when the occasion arose. Men slept on the ground floor, the night rooms for women and children were above. There were no external windows, light and ventilation being provided through narrow gratings that overlooked the yards. Integral quarters for the keeper and his wife consisted of a parlour, scullery and pantry, and chambers above. They drew water from a well. The prisoners cooked or heated their food on open fires in the day rooms, the only source of warmth against the cold. The prison garden lay beyond the walls.

Mixing together the young and old, those awaiting trial, the debtors and the felons, remained less than satisfactory. Those in a filthy condition could not be bathed; those who were clean could not wash. There was no provision for the infirm or separate cells for troublesome inmates. The rooms were small with ceilings only seven feet high. Pressure on the accommodation obliged the justices to have the garret lined for the sick.

The prison administration became more ordered. Isaac Wood, the keeper in 1773 and later to become master of the county gaol in Lincoln, was directed to make a record of all those committed to the prison. Name, age and place of nativity, and a short description of their person was to be entered in a book provided for the purpose, together with the name and abode of the magistrate committing them. These records have not survived. In addition he was to provide a calendar, or list, of all those detained in the prison and produced at sessions.

In October that year the justices ordered that *Mary Reed, a dumb vagrant woman be detained and employed in the House of Correction at Louth till next sessions or until her place of settlement was ascertained or she can provide for herself.*

From April 1772 the justices required the presence of constables in court to keep order and regulate proceedings. Disorder and lawlessness within the population was creeping into court. To endorse their authority, 24 wands (truncheons or staffs) were purchased to assist the constables and bailiff in keeping order.

American independence in 1776 brought an abrupt end to transportation. Within ten years unfortunates and ne'er-do-wells filled the nation's prisons to overflowing. Poor conditions grew worse, and a movement for penal reform took hold. The punishment of offenders was about to change, but not necessarily for the better.

> October 6th 1767
> A Calender for South Sessions
>
> Francis Whittingham, Charg'd upon Oath, by Will'm Lawson for threatning to knock out his Eyes, Committed by Justice Finley Clerk.
> *Recommitted to next Quarter Sessions*
>
> Mary Wilson, Charg'd for Stealing one Coverlid for a Bed, one Warming pan and Six Trenchers, and for being a Lewd disorderly Woman Committed by Matthew Lister Esq.
> *Discharged*

Sessions Calendar 1767
Prepared by the keeper every quarter, these lists later named all inmates of the House of Correction.
Lindsey Quarter Sessions Records A/1/158/40
Lincolnshire Archives Office

- 4 -

Sloth and Debauchery

JOHN Howard was appointed High Sheriff of Bedfordshire in 1773. Having inherited his father's estates by the age of 47 he was a wealthy country gentleman. Required to sit as a justice in his own courts, he was appalled at the condition of many of the prisoners appearing before him: sallow, meagre countenances, covered, hardly covered, in rags. Shocked by the unsanitary condition he found on a visit to Bedford jail, he travelled to prisons in the surrounding counties to learn how best to improve the lot of the inmates. He found their plight to be no better, and undertook to survey and report upon the state of the prisons, and their occupants, to Parliament.

At the time there were more than 250 jails in England and Wales. Howard estimated the prison population as 4,375, of whom about half were debtors. A quarter of the prisons had less than 10 inmates. At Lincoln there were barely 50, and then only at the time of the twice yearly assize. Only in London were there jails with more than a hundred behind bars: Newgate for the felons, Clerkenwell Bridewell for the petty offenders, and the King's Bench, Marshalsea and Fleet prisons for debtors.

Howard estimated the numbers confined in the prisons of England and Wales:

	In 1779	In 1782
Debtors Men	1,959	2,058
Debtors Women -	119	139
Felons -	798	991
Petty Offenders -	917	1,017
Prisoners in the hulks -	526	204
Supposed omitted -	60	30
Total number of prisoners	4,379	4,439

A small allowance was made for the corporation prisons not visited, and convicts on the hulks awaited transportation. The prison population today approaches 72,000.

Apart from the county gaols, used mainly for the assize prisoners, and the responsibility of the sheriff, there were two types of prison, the common gaols and the houses of correction.

Common gaols were run as businesses. They were places of custody for individuals awaiting trial and retribution. Detention was not thought of as part of the punishment. The gaoler's purpose was to prevent the prisoner's escape, and to make a profit. There were charges for the cell, a bed – or part of one, food, clothes and the fitting and removal of irons. Even those acquitted by the courts were not discharged until they had paid their fees. If they could not pay, they became debtors, and were kept in prison. The wealthy might expect favours from their captors but were more likely subject to extortion. For the poor, there was nothing.

Conditions in the houses of correction were more closely linked to local justices, who appointed the master and paid him a salary. Inevitably the distinction between the two was slowly eroded. Whilst the justices of the peace remained responsible for sentences served, scant steps were taken to ensure the well being of those detained.

Howard found few prisons supplied with the necessities of life. Water was often fetched on a daily basis by the keeper. Each prisoner was allowed three pints a day, barely enough to drink, let alone keep themselves clean. In many bridewells there was no allowance for food, the prisoners' own labour expected to maintain them. Without tools or materials there was little work. Inmates begged through the gratings, spending their days in *sloth, profanities and debauchery to an extremely shocking degree.*

Day rooms and courts were shared, with men and women only separated at night. Idiots, lunatics and the insane served as sport or, if not kept separate, disturbed and terrified the other prisoners. At night all were crowded into the sleeping wards, 14 to 16 hours between dusk and dawn in wintertime. Damp rags served as bedding. Straw, if not an extra to be paid for, was only replaced as it turned to dust. Windows were stopped up to avoid the window tax, making the air in the close rooms *feculant and noxious*.

Howard was moved to record that *the air made poisonous by the effluvia of the sick and whatever else in prisons is so offensive … in my first journeys my clothes were so offensive that in a post-chaise I could not bear the windows drawn up, and was therefore obliged to travel on horse back. I did not wonder … many gaolers made excuses and did not go with me into the felons ward.*

In such conditions sickness and disease, especially the dread gaol distemper – probably typhus – might wreck havoc. At the Black Assize

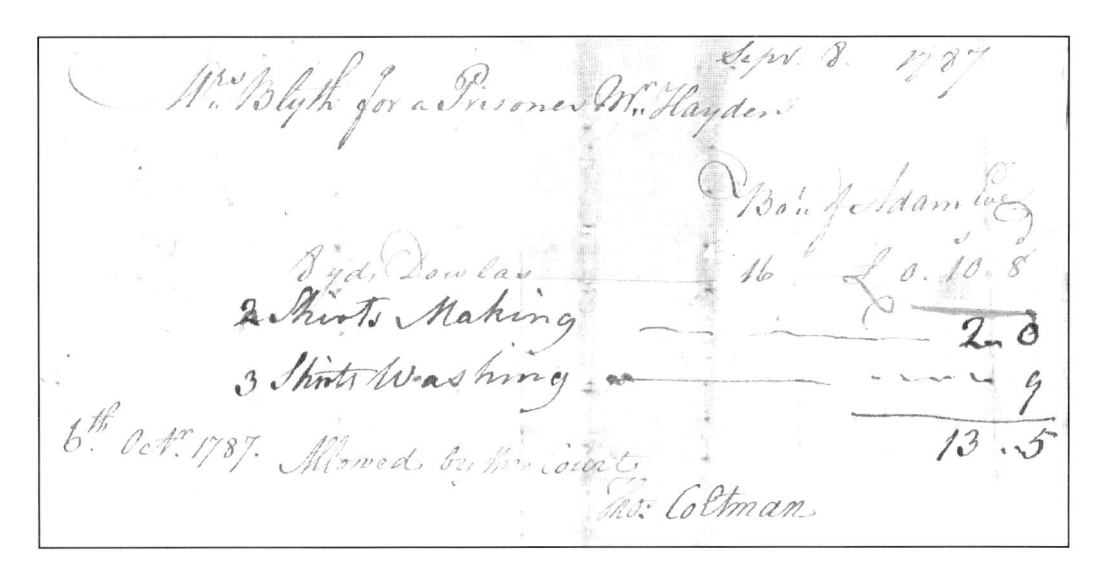

Clothing for the destitute
Vagrants in rags were supplied with second hand boots and clothes, bought in for that purchase. 'Washing' was most unusual.
Lindsey Quarter Sessions Records A/1/238/88
Lincolnshire Archives Office

in Oxford Castle in 1577, 300 died in 40 hours, including the Lord Chief Justice Baron. In 1730, prisoners from Ilchester gaol took the fever to the Lent assize at Taunton. The Chief Justice, his Sergeant, the County Sheriff and a hundred others perished as a result of the gaol distemper. Depleted by war with the French in Canada, His Majesty's service required a speedy supply of seafaring men for the fleet. A bounty of 20 shillings was offered for each fit seaman, and 6d a mile travel. Impressed men carried the gaol fever into the army and the fleet, where the guard ships took the distemper into the squadrons, resulting in the loss of 2,000 men in the American war.

Howard believed that a term of imprisonment might be used to both punish and reform the delinquent. He advised less brutal alternatives to hanging and transportation, especially for less serious breaches of the law. A sentence of two to three years detention might provide offenders, detained in separate cells and sleeping alone, with time to reflect upon their wrongdoings. He advocated the construction of large penitentiaries where the different classes of prisoner could be segregated one from another in their own cells, where fees were not payable to the gaoler, and with separate wards for the sick and infirm. Cleanliness and improved ventilation were important to prevent the spread of disease. Running water and baths should be freely available. The keeper should be paid a salary, with no interest in the sale of liquor to his charges, and an apothecary or surgeon, and a chaplain should be appointed for the inmates' welfare. Local magistrates should make regular visits to inspect the prison and report upon its management. In the meantime existing gaols and houses of correction needed to be improved.

John Howard's presentation of evidence to Parliament resulted in laws intended to improve the lot of the prisoner's health. Without administration to enforce their will, or inspection to report upon its effect, little was achieved immediately at local level.

Reform, if it was recognised as such in Lindsey, was exceeding slow. At the end of 1774, William Blythe, *Keeper of His Majesty's Prison, the House of Correction at Louth*, laid a written report before the magistrates describing the prison's lack of capacity. Most importantly to him there was no separate ward for the persons committed for small debts. He was obliged to lodge, confine and victual them with felons and trespassers. Since they were entitled to the tools of their trade, a more liberal diet, and freedom of visits by relatives, the debtor's friends threatened him with prosecution. He described himself as a poor man with a wife and eight children to support. His salary of £37 5s 4d a year was barely adequate. If he had known the numbers in his care would increase so he would not have accepted the post.

He recommended the prison be enlarged and asked that his salary be increased accordingly. Little was done. When William Blythe died in 1782, his son John was appointed in his place.

As a result of the *Act for preserving the Health of Prisoners and preventing the Gaol Distemper*, the justices ordered the walls and ceilings of the cells and wards of the felons, and any other rooms used by prisoners in the House of Correction at Louth, to be scraped and whitewashed at least once a year. The buildings were to be constantly supplied with fresh air. A copy of the Act was to be *painted in large and legible Characters upon a Board, and hung up in some conspicuous part of the said House of Correction.* Louth prison walls were heightened, though the yard gate and the fencing on the east side of the garden remained in bad repair.

Magistrates were appointed to visit the prison and appraise the conditions they found. They generally reported 'All's well'. Their colleagues in the castle at Lincoln use similar terms.

From the Lincoln minute book we read: *22 July. We have visited the gaol and find everything in good order. We think it right to remark that in the Passage leading to the Watch Tower we found two baskets, one containing bones of Convicts who had been executed and the other some ropes used for the purposes of execution. We recommend that the bones be buried and the ropes destroyed.*

The appointment of Thomas Hardy as Doctor of Physic to the prisoners in Louth brought them some benefits. The treatment of prisoners for minor ailments provided a steady income for the post-holder. Lotion, liniment, oil and drops, linctus, aniseed, and cream of

		£ s d
	Brought Forward	4 18 7
	Drawing a tooth (Coachman)	" " 6
28	A Pot of Ointment (Ferdinand)	" 1 0
	An Opening Electuary	" 1 -
	Ointment & Lint	" " 6
April 9	Bleeding Mrs B	" " 6
	Bleeding Old Nelly	" " 6
	Bleeding (Ferdinand)	" " 6
	A Balsamic Electuary	" 1 2
	Bleeding (Smith)	" " 6
	a Vomit &c (Coachman)	" 1 -
14	a Vomit &c (Paste)	" 1 -
	Spanish Juice	" " 6
	The Electuary (Ferdinand)	" 1 2
		£ 5 9 11

April 21. 1792
South Sessions } Allowed by the Court

Thos. Ulman &c

Bleeding Old Nelly
The sick were a profitable source of income for appointed surgeons, often one of the Justices.
Lindsey Quarter Sessions A/1/256/44
Lincolnshire Archives Office

> Louth 6th Octor 1786
>
> We - The Grand Jury present that a Chamber in the House of Correction (which is now useless) be fitted up that a proper Pump be put down and that a Stone Cistern for the Purpose of Bathing be placed in the Prison. The Prison Yard to be paved with Pebbles and the low Cell to be boarded, and the Brick Cell to have a Chimney in it.
>
> Samʳ Welfitt Foreman

Lindsey Quarter Sessions Records A/1/234/36
Lincolnshire Achives Office

tartar, cinnamon water, white vitriol and spirits of wine were used, and treatments were charged at two or three shillings a time, sometimes more, half a day's wages for a labouring man. With salts and emetics, saffron and Spanish juice, tinctures of myrtle and rhubarb, oil of almonds and solvalotile also on the list, it was little wonder that some also needed an 'opening mixture'. Provided the surgeon saw the patient before prescribing treatment, he was obliged to consider conditions within the gaol. At least some members of the well to do were brought face to face with the lives of the poor and to recognise their plight.

Elsewhere the justices agreed the sum of £42 9s 6d for the construction of a temporary house of correction at Alford. This resolved the expense of detaining prisoners in public houses until examined and brought to Louth. At Gainsborough they adjourned to the White Hart Inn. They decided that an Act requiring clergymen to officiate to all prisoners was only desirous in the county gaol on account of the small number of prisoners confined elsewhere.

Howard was not satisfied with the response to his findings, and spent the next 16 years travelling the country, and much of Europe, speaking for reform. Amongst others he visited the county bridewells at Folkingham for the Parts of Kesteven, Spalding for the Parts of Holland, and the town gaols at Boston and Stamford.

Standards varied considerably. Perhaps one of the worst in the county was the Lincoln city gaol at the Stonebow Gate. Two rooms for male and female debtors were upstairs. For criminals, two dungeons, one a cage for close confinement, were reached down three steps. They were so damp that occupants were provided with bedsteads to keep them off the ground, but no water or straw. Nor was there an exercise court. Thankfully there were few inmates, normally less than five. Fees were payable to the keeper: a shilling (5p) a week for a bed, four shillings and sixpence (22p) for a weeks 'lodging' and three meals a day, and three shillings and four pence (17p) payable on discharge (twice that amount for a debtor).

The prison at Spalding was comparatively new, with three airy rooms, two of them with a fireplace, and a workroom 28 feet long. Prisoners were not permitted access to water at the pump as the exercise courtyard was not secure.

At Folkingham there were five damp rooms beneath the keeper's house, with access through a trap door in one of them to the dungeon. The small court was without water or sewer. There were few prisoners, a lunatic being the only long term resident. At Stamford Town Hall were two cells and a debtors room, where prisoners were charged one shilling and four pence a day for their food and lodging, and a shilling a week for cleaning their room. The smithy was paid two shillings if irons (shackles) were used or removed, and there was 6d for the person carrying out the sentences of pillory, burning in the hand or whipping.

The County gaol at the castle in Lincoln was rented from the Duchy of Lancaster. Without a salary, the gaoler was dependent on allowances, fees, and the sale of beer to the inmates. The keeper brewed the beer himself in the taproom next to his apartments on the ground floor. Accommodation for the debtors was on the floor above, fairly spacious but not very clean. A trap door in one of their rooms allowed access to the rest of the prison below. For male prisoners there were two vaulted, dirty and offensive dungeons. One, referred to as the Pit, measured 14 feet by 21 feet with one small window 2 feet by 14 inches. Next to it was the condemned cell, one-third the size with an even smaller window, and a little chopped straw on the floor. A sizeable day room, 15 feet by 19 feet, and separate wards for the women felons. Debtors were allowed to provide their own beds and bedding, and have the necessaries of life brought in to them. Their ale was restricted to no more than a quart a day to prevent disturbances. For debtors who did not behave well, a room was set aside for their close confinement. For other prisoners, eight pounds of wholesome household bread and one pound weight of beef were delivered weekly. Admission, discharge, food and lodging were all chargeable. Two shillings and sixpence garnish or pot money was a bounty payable by the prisoner on admission, supposedly for the benefit of the other inmates, and probably used to purchase their liquor. One shilling and three pence was charged for a bed, double if prisoners wanted the whole bed to themselves. If the gaoler thought fit, a felon's irons could be removed for two shillings and sixpence a week, *but gentlemen and the better sort of criminal* paid five shillings. There was no water or sewer, and the prison was neglected and in poor repair.

Howard's work is not acknowledged as such in the minutes of the Lindsey justices. Parliament's concern that many places of detention were not suitable for the long term custody of prisoners resulted in the appointment of a committee to consider the suitability of the prison at Gainsborough, where the difficulty of keeping the men and women separate, and the lack of a strong room for desperate persons was addressed, and at Louth, which the justices thought sufficient, provided minor repairs and alterations were carried through. The wall was raised and topped with wooden spikes, and the keeper authorised to purchase ten jersey wheels. The prisoners were to be kept occupied by spinning and combing wool.

The court remained reluctant to use imprisonment as a punishment. Neither Louth nor Gainsborough had sufficient capacity. Enlargement and renewal of the buildings, and the subsequent long term care of the inmates, would prove expensive. It was cheaper to leave things as they were.

John Grant was a grazier living with his wife and grown-up children at Withcall. In spring 1784 the family employed a number of servants. One of these, Rebecca Bolton, a young married woman, was not content with her lot and left her service at about four o'clock one morning in May. When the household realised she was missing, it became apparent she had taken with her items of clothing that were not hers. A cotton gown, an apron and a silk handkerchief belonging to the Grants could not be found.

When Rebecca Bolton failed to return and explain her conduct, the Grants were obliged to take action. A servant who stole from the person who employed them expected to be punished if they were caught. An employer could not be seen as a weak disciplinarian. The Grants travelled to Louth where they told the magistrate what had happened. Bentley Bennett Esq., a local justice of the peace, took written depositions and issued a warrant for Rebecca Bolton's arrest.

Ponies were hired and constables despatched to apprehend her. She was detained and brought first to Keddington, then on to Louth. In her voluntary confession to Bennett she admitted the theft of her master's property and also to the taking of a black silk hat and handkerchief, a length of ribbon and a pair of leather shoes belonging to Lucy Holmes and Margaret Waltham, two of the other servants. She was handed into the care of the keeper of the Louth House of Correction to await her trial.

Two months later at the July, or Thomas-a-Beckett, sessions, the grand jury found there was a case, or True Bill, to answer for petty larceny (where the goods were valued at under a shilling). Convicted of felony she was liable to burning in the hand or whipping. The court ordered her transported for the term of seven years, *as soon as conveniently may be*, to one of His Majesty's colonies or plantations in America.

Few records remain to help us with the details of what, to the courts, was a fairly minor matter. John Grant, the head of the family, was no stranger to the process of law. At the Easter sessions in Louth that year he prosecuted David Brattley, a labourer from Donington on Bain for larceny, for which offence the man was sentenced to one month's imprisonment.

Jonathen Merriken, named as a witness, was bound over on the sum of £10 to attend Rebecca Bolton's trial and give evidence, but his deposition has not survived.

On the face of it the facts are fairly conclusive, but they might also support a different interpretation. Rebecca Bolton would be expected to rise early as a servant. There were fires to light and water to heat, and food to prepare and cook for the household. As a yeoman grazier, John Grant needed to make the most of every daylight hour, and the household needed to be up and working. If they wished to display their wealth, servants needed to be well presented in case of visitors or errands to town, and were likely to be provided with a suit of clothes. If Rebecca Bolton ran away in the clothes she stood up in, she was at risk of being charged with their theft, as with the paupers absconding from the Workhouse. The date of the offence is a little unsettling as it coincides with the annual hiring fairs for labour at the beginning of May. She would be unlikely to spoil a year's good work record by running away so close to the end of her service, or to leave a new employment so quickly.

Rebecca Bolton had been before the magistrates in February earlier that year for stealing a shift and petticoat at Stickney. She must have been aware of the risk she was taking of another conviction, yet her life was so poor and meaningless that the likelihood of transportation or hanging held no deterrent for her. That her sentence was no longer possible because of American independence seems to have been of little consideration. Justices were appointed to oversee the contract and she was returned to the House of Correction to await transfer to the county gaol in the castle at Lincoln.

As more convicts were sentenced to transportation, the prisons quickly became overcrowded, and old ships or hulks moored along the Thames or on the south coast were used to provide additional accommodation. Central government needed to find somewhere quickly to empty the prisons, and after some controversy decided to use the isolated continent of Australia as a dumping ground. Cook had charted the coast in 1772 and Sir Joseph Banks had recommended

Botany Bay as a suitable destination.

Whilst awaiting her fate, Rebecca Bolton gave birth to a baby girl, and in March 1787, nearly three years after her conviction, a turnkey from Lincoln gaol delivered Rebecca and her daughter to the transport ship *Prince of Wales* moored off Portsmouth harbour. The First Fleet (as it later became known) set sail on the 13th May 1787 for the colony in New South Wales. There were 11 ships in all, two navy ships, three store ships and six transports, with officers, marines, crew and nearly 800 convicts. The gaols of the land were scoured in a desperate attempt to provide 200 women convicts to redress the imbalance of the sexes.

Botany Bay proved disappointing, and the fleet moved a few miles north to Sidney Cove. Disembarkation of the sorry cargo began at the end of January 1788. Rebecca Bolton did not survive to tell her tale but died within three months of landing in Australia. Her daughter, not yet two years old, was buried a week later.

"The Warrior" Convict-hulk, Woolwich
Illustrated London News,   February 1846
Local Studies Library,   Lincoln

- 5 -

Against the Peace

THERE is little evidence to suggest the justices of Lindsey were sufficiently influenced by Howard's works to feel a sudden compassion for their charges. As a result of delays experienced in the transportation of convicts, and greater use of the jails as places of punishment, the prison population increased beyond the existing capacity. The justices, finding themselves obliged to review the present accommodation, and plan for the future, were brought in direct contact with the wretched lives of the inmates.

In April 1785, the keeper at Lincoln, Isaac Wood, made representations to the Grand Jury that the castle gaol *was very ruinous, broken and in great decay, and by reason thereof is wholly insufficient and unsafe for the due keeping and securing of Felons and other prisoners.* A panel of justices were nominated to consider what action to take, and £500 set aside in anticipation of the cost. Their findings supported Wood's claim. A new county gaol was planned, to be constructed using convict labour from the old prison at an estimated cost £7,000.

At Louth the House of Correction was to be improved and extended as the need arose, but in 1786 conditions were much as they had been 30 years before. Development was exceeding slow, and the buildings were slipping into decay. Allowed three pence a day to keep the prisoners, the keeper sometimes provided additional bread on Sundays.

The sale of spirituous liquor to prisoners in the county was brought to an end two years later. Considerable compensation was paid to the gaolers in lieu of the profits lost to them. Isaac Wood at the castle was allowed £200 in addition to his salary, an aberration perhaps by the justices, though only trimmed back slightly the following year. An indication of the importance to the keeper's income of charges made on the prisoners.

In spring 1789 the justices turned their attention to the larger of the two gaols in Lindsey, the House of Correction in Gainsborough, where

25 prisoners filled the gaol. Men outnumbered women prisoners about three to one, but were now lodged in separate rooms. With ceilings no more than seven feet high, all wards were small and less than 15 feet square.

On the day of the justices visit to the gaol, 11 men were crowded together in the day room, *dark, close, smoky and so extremely offensive as to be scarcely supportable*. At night the same prisoners slept in a slightly larger lodging room. A third ward was given over to the sole use of two ungovernable and refractory inmates. A staircase took up much of the women's day room, and gave access to their chambers on the floor above. Of the three women in residence, one was insane.

Two exercise yards 33 feet square, two workshops with blocks and hammers, and a solitary cell completed the prison buildings. There was no water, or places to bath, wash or clean. The bridewell rooms were short of hemp, handmills or looms for the purposes of labour. The prison lacked provision for the sick, diseased or filthy. *Vice and profligacy was increased*. There was no hope. The gaoler confessed that for some time past the inmates' conduct had given rise to alarm and apprehension. He confessed himself unable to keep them in order, restrain, or employ them. The justices noted the appearance of the prisoners to be forlorn, desperate and abandoned. The committee viewed with great concern *so large a number of their fellow creatures thus confined together*. At last it seemed the justices were beginning to acknowledge their responsibilities.

They allowed that the old prison buildings were no longer adequate and recommended the construction of a new general bridewell and sessions house at Kirton. The site was central to the district of west Lindsey, and about six miles north of the old sessions court at Spital. The court and prison at Gainsborough, and the security risk entailed when transferring prisoners over long distances, and the alternate sessions house at Caistor, sinking into the ground and so damp as to be a health risk, would become surplus to requirements. They thought their choice an expensive option, but hoped the sale of the prison in such a busy market town as Gainsborough would bear a good price. To differentiate between the two, the prison at Louth was always referred to as the House of Correction, the jail at Kirton as the bridewell.

Records kept by the courts show little change in attitudes towards punishment and retribution. However it is doubtful that Eleanor Coupland thought she had been treated with any special leniency.

Theophilus Benton was a shop man for George White of Alford. On the Saturday before Christmas 1788, he was minding the general store in Willoughby. The shop was rented from Richard Wood, a yeoman farmer, who lived next door. Shortly after seven o'clock that evening Eleanor Coupland called at the shop. She was a labourer's wife and lived in the village. Theophilus Benton knew her well, and they were on friendly terms. He watched as she made her way to a corner of the store. He was perturbed when he saw her place her hand in a bag of candles and then to the pocket of her dress. He suspected she had stolen something. Being uncertain as to what he should do he went next door and spoke to Mrs Wood, the farmer's wife. Asked whether she thought he should proceed against her or reprimand her, she advised the latter.

Theophilus returned to the store and called Eleanor into the yard where Mary Wood heard him say, "Nelly, I am afraid you have taken something from me". Upon being so reproached, Eleanor Coupland took from her pocket a pound of candles and gave them up to the shopman, assuring him she had taken nothing else, and offered to submit to a search. Unfortunately the matter did not rest with a talking-to for the miscreant.

Written depositions about the incident are taken from Theophilus and other witnesses a week later by a local magistrate. The wording of the statements hints that neither was happy with the process of the law. Eleanor Coupland was arrested, brought to Louth and charged with theft, and lodged in the House of Correction.

On 13th January she was amongst other prisoner taken to Spilsby to appear at the quarter sessions, shackled with others in an open cart or wagon, and escorted by constables on horseback, something of a local spectacle. On a previous occasion the keeper of the House of Correction had been commended for bringing the prisoners to Spilsby through the snow, and awarded twenty shillings extra expenses.

Brought before the court for stealing one pound weight of candles, valued at 6d, the property of George White, she pleaded not guilty. The Grand Jury considered there was evidence for a True Bill against her, and the case was called before the petty jury for their decision. This was a simple case, quickly decided. After hearing the evidence of the witnesses the jury found her guilty, and the justices passed sentence: *To be recommitted to the House of Correction at Louth till Monday 16th February next to be then brought to Spilsby, the next day taken to Alford and there publickly Whipt from the prison round the Sheep Market to the Church Yard Gate, and from thence to the Water and back again to the prison through the Market Place and there discharged.* For six pennyworth of candles at Christmas.

Six weeks in the House of Correction. Stripped to the waist in the middle of February, hands tied to the back of a cart, hauled through the town on market day and given 30 to 40 lashes. Two shillings and sixpence for whomsoever gave the whipping. Punishment, reform or humiliation? What encouragement for Theophilus Benton.

Being old and decayed, the prison buildings in Louth were proving to be high maintenance and a source of income for several local traders. The quarterly accounts show a constant expenditure on bricks, lime, mortar and horse hair for rebuilding the walls; sand, gravel and paving for the yards; timber, nails and oak posts to repair fencing and gates; glass and lead work for the glazier to renew dozens of squares of broken panes of glass; carpentry for broken doors and bedsteads, and iron work for the smithy for the damaged locks, cranks, bolts and bands, 'hould' fasts and double jointed handcuffs, bars and spikes for the windows, and the riveting and removal of irons. Hints perhaps of a high rate of attrition on the structure of the building by discontented and fractious occupants.

There was no book of rules, but once a year the justices required the keeper to certify the prison was conducted in accordance to their directions. John Blythe's certificate was the response in the second column:

A copy of the fees and rules to be hung up -	A copy shall be hung up
Felons and debtors to be kept separate -	As separate as room will admit
No spirituous liquors in the gaol -	No such thing allowed
Clergymen may officiate in gaols -	No Clergyman attends the house of correction
Persons discharged through want of prosecution to be discharged without fee -	No fee shall be charged by me
Cells to be lime washed once a year -	It shall be done
The Cells shall be kept clean -	The Cells are Kept clean
They shall be supplied with fresh air by Ventilators -	There are no Ventilators
There shall be two rooms set apart for the sick -	The Prison will not admit two rooms for the sick
That a warm or cold bath or Bathing tubs shall be provided -	There is none for use in the prison
A surgeon or apothecary shall be appointed -	Wrigglesworth and Wilson attend the prison

The gaoler's response varied little year on year, but the justices made no changes.

The inmates of the gaol were usually the impoverished of society. Those prisoners previously in employment were most likely labourers

A Bill of Expences for Jane Nixon who
Remains yet Sick

		£	s	d
Sepr. 12th 1787 Orderd by Mr Wuggelsworth half a Pint of Wine Every Day			11	6
half a tb of Sugar Every Day			5	9
6 Strike of Coals			3	3
Candle			6	-
Mutton for Broth twice			1	0
a Woman Sitting up with her one Week Every Night			3	6
The Womans Supper & Breakfast & Ale			4	0
Bed 3 Weeks			4	6
		£1	14	0
2 Quarts of Vinegar			1	0
For Bringing Thos. Smith from Spilsby Sessions last by Order of Court 10 Mile at 1/ pr. Mile			15	8
			10	0

6th Octr. 1787. Allowed by the Court   £2 .. 13 .. 0

Thos. Coltman

Medical Expenses
Care of the sick entailed considerable expense. A nurse is hired for Jane Nixon.
Wine in the diet was usually a bad sign.
Lindsey Quarter Sessions Records A/1/238/85
Lincolnshire Archives Office

or servants. Life in the House of Correction could be an unpleasant and threatening experience. Many were destitute, families of the travelling poor - often with children, vagrants and beggars. The justices were convinced that those travelling without passes were being encouraged to enter Lincolnshire by the constables and powers that be of towns and parishes beyond the Humber. This may well have been so. In consequence they erected a sign at Barton Waterside warning all *Vagrants who shall enter this Division without a legal pass will be immediately apprehended and dealt with according to law.* To add effect to the warning table, a whipping post was set next to the landing stage. Welcome to the Parts of Lindsey.

Lincolnshire remained a region whose people continued to work on the land. The first census in 1801 recorded a population of 209,000. Louth, the principal town in the north-east of the county, had grown to just over 4,000 inhabitants. Farming remained a most important occupation. By the turn of the 19th century, most of the open fields and commons had been enclosed. The costs of enclosure worked to the benefit of the more wealthy landowners, and ownership of some parishes in Lindsey, especially on the Wolds, fell into the hands of a few individuals. The loss of the commons was of particular importance to the poor. The subsistence living they had been able to scratch from the woods and grazing was no longer available to them.

Weakened by their labours, and with limited or no access to a nourishing diet, many detained in prison were in poor physical condition. They became vulnerable to illness and contagious disease, but had little access to medical care. In Louth, treatment for the sick by the apothecary or surgeon in the House of Correction supplemented assistance available under the Poor Laws. For those the surgeon deemed in poor health, the daily allowance for the keeper of the House was doubled. Three pence a day for the prisoners became sixpence a day for the sick, and may have entailed an enhanced diet. Costs for the seriously ill could escalate, especially if the prison was obliged to board a nurse. Over three months, treatment for a dumb man doubled from seven to 14 shillings a week. When all failed, there was crape for the corpse, a coffin, bearers and burial fees.

When infants were born in the House there were charges for 'laying in': three weeks board for a nurse, and clothing for the child. The apothecary often directed the keeper to find garments for inmates: bed gowns, shirts, stockings, breeches, an apron, shoes and handkerchiefs. A week's bed and a fire might be prescribed. There were teeth to draw, bodies to be bled, and ointment for the itch, sago and pearl barley to be supplied, and 'plaisters' for the knee.

The expense of maintaining the inmates was high, and the keeper's allowance of three pence a day for caring for the prisoners was under pressure. Crop failures of the 1790s that brought about the

Speenhamland system for relief of the poor (their payments were linked to the price of corn) also raised the costs of correction. The keeper's allowance for prisoners increased to two shillings and four pence a week, and doubled again if they were ill.

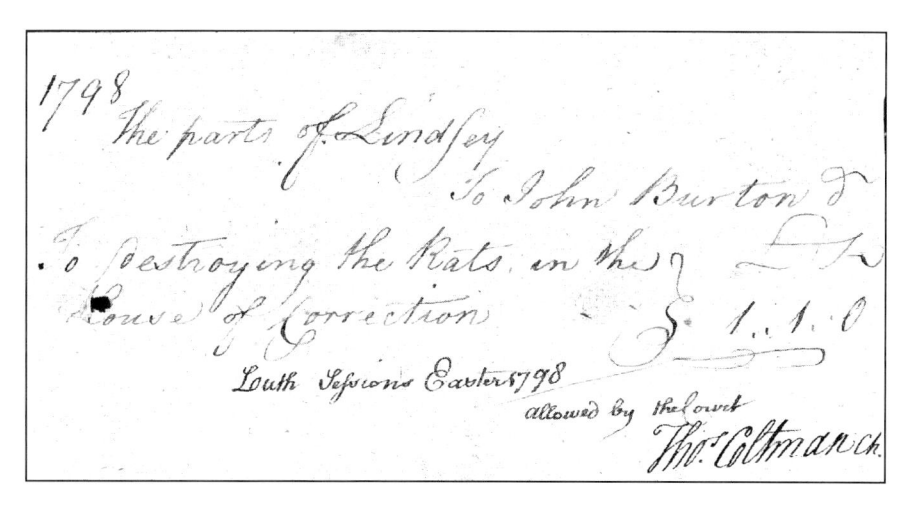

Rats in the House
Lindsey Quarter Sessions A/1/280/37
Lincolnshire Archives Office

The four chimneys were swept every quarter, the yards were brushed clean with birch besoms, there were cauldrons of coal for the fires, and straw for a year's bedding cost a guinea. There was work for the rat catcher.

From the *Hue and Cry, and Police Gazette* 26 October 1799: *Escaped from the House of Correction at Louth, Lincolnshire on the night of the 6th October. William Coggle, late of Legbourne, near Louth, a Deserter from the 5th Regiment of Foot, about 34 Years of Age, and 5 feet 6 inches high, and has since his Desertion cut all the Toes from his left Foot, which is now well, had on a Velveret Jacket and Breeches, Striped Waistcoat, a Pair of Brown Worsted Stockings, a Strong Pair of Shoes and Steel Buckles, and when in Liquor is fond of Singing. Whoever will Apprehend the above described Person and Lodge him in one of His Majesty's Gaols, and give information thereof to Thomas Waddington, Keeper of the said House of Correction, shall receive a reward of Five Guineas, beside all Reasonable Charges.*

Three other men also breached the wall that night.

Smallpox was in the House over Christmas. The Easter quarter sessions in Louth give a fair indication of the administration of justice at the turn of the century, the 40th year of the reign of George III.

The court met in the town hall on the south side of the Market Place. Too small for its purpose, the building was old and in poor repair, and was in a noisy situation. Four justices were present, as required for the trial of felons, under the chairmanship of Thomas Coltman, the town Warden. They assembled to consider various felonies, trespasses and misdemeanours committed against the peace of their said Lord, the King. The justices had no legal training, and relied upon their clerk, Joseph Brackenbury, for guidance as to the law.

The bailiff was responsible for the conduct of the court. He was dressed in a long blue coat and waistcoat trimmed with gold lace, a pair of black velveteen trousers, and a top hat. He was the only one present in any form of uniform. He separated the panel of 36 jurymen. The grand jury, those of more advanced age, extensive property or higher station in life retired to the jury room above. The petty jurors comprised the remaining twelve.

A chief constable and four or five petty, or parish, constable were on duty to assist the bailiff in maintaining order in the court and prevent the escape of prisoners. There were about a dozen accused, including several women, in the courtroom, or the cells below, brought in fetters from the House of Correction by the keeper earlier that morning.

The minutes of a later sessions recorded that *the distance from the Court house in Louth and the want of a gaol in Spilsby have hitherto been reasons for taking all the prisoners together into Court and keeping them there during the whole Time of the Sessions, they have been always from the their sores, their Diseases and other Complaints offensive, sometimes unwholesome, and the effluvia from them frequently alarming in a small hot crowded court.*

The court was further crowded with witnesses surrendering to their bail, attorneys and their clients, and the friends (and enemies) of those to be charged with offences.

Whilst the grand jury considered written evidence taken in cases to be heard later, the business of the court began. Thomas Roe, a clerk from Horncastle and religious dissenter, swore his allegiance to the crown, and William Moyses and William Bee produced references and took the woolwinders' oath. A fine on the parishioners of Scremby, Grebby and Great Steeping, who had failed to repair their highways, was delayed to another session, as was a similar case against the inhabitants of Covenham Saint Mary, who failed to appear.

Joseph Spence, a wheelwright from Wragby was brought before the justices. As the father of Ann Nuttal's child he was expected to contribute towards the cost of its upbringing. Provided he did so, no action would be taken. Ann Nuttal, from Utterby, would only find herself in court, and thence the House of Correction, if she abandoned the child to the parish. Five other men also had bastardy orders confirmed against them, but an appeal by John Bamber that he was not the father of Mary Smith's infant was respited, or put back, to the next sessions.

> To the worshipful the Justices who sit at South Sessions
>
> This is to certify that My Parishioner Mr John Warter is so indisposed by sickness, that he cannot attend upon the Jury, the ensuing Session.
>
> Witness my hand John Dunkley, Minister
>
> Kirkstead October 4th 1781

Sick Note
Jurors at Lindsey were expected to stand throughout court proceedings. 'Bad legs' was a fair excuse. Failure to attend without reason resulted in a fine for the juror and possibly the constable directed to warn him.
Lindsey Quarter Sessions A/1/214/50
Lincolnshire Archives Office

Elizabeth Stephenson, the wife of a soldier serving with the militia, the second Regiment of Foot, contested an order removing her and her six-year old daughter, Ann, from Haltham upon Bain to Horncastle. A decision was adjourned to a later date.

An officer sought judgement and directions on the disposal of foreign spirits - 190 gallons - seized by the Excise. Richard Cheffins from Willoughby had been selling tobacco without a licence, and James and Charles Dickinson, who found a seaman's chest on the beach at Ingoldmells and kept the contents, were being pursued by the Lord of the Manor who claimed the property as his.

In the meantime the grand jury had completed their deliberations and found True Bills in all cases except one. They decided the evidence against Robert Dabb for stealing oats, barley and beans was insufficient to warrant a prosecution, there was no bill to answer, and he was discharged.

The petty jury tried the remaining cases. All the defendants pleaded 'not guilty'. David Souden, a farmer, was charged with assault and battery upon the body of Rhodia Epton from Mumby cum Chapel. Robert Hewer, a surgeon from Alford, gave evidence in the case, but there were no other witnesses apart from the victim, a labourer's wife. The jury found Souden not guilty.

Three witnesses were called in the next case, against Susanna Parker, a servant girl from Hatton. She had called at a draper's shop in

Horncastle, and told the proprietor that her mistress had sent her to buy some material. She selected a print for a gown, a red cloak and a pair of gloves, and lengths of ribbon and muslin. Mr. Scott believed they would be paid for later. The goods were wrapped and Parker took them from the shop. The lady of the house had no knowledge of the purchase, and the jury convicted the accused of a false pretence. She was sent to the bridewell in the new prison at Kirton for 12 months.

Jonathan Chapman, a farmer, was also sentenced to 12 months in the bridewell at Kirton for stealing hay, but not before he had been whipped from the town hall to the church and back again on market day.

Goose Pies in the Oven
*The examination of Mary Slater shows
the victim of crime instigating a court appearance.*
**Lindsey Quarter Sessions Record A/1/111/3
Lincolnshire Archives Office**

It seems possible that the next defendant, widow Mary Short, had reason to harbour a grudge against a family at Tattershall Thorpe. In August the previous year the Richardsons had been victims of a number of thefts, damage and arson. Considerable effort and expense had been incurred in attempting a prosecution. In the absence of a police force, the Richardsons were required to assemble the case and bring the suspect to court. Before an arrest warrant could be issued, witnesses were required to be taken before a magistrate to swear a written statement, and there was transport to arrange to the nearest town - horses, a cart and a man to drive, food, ale and lodgings to pay for and justices' fees and a retainer for the attorney and his clerk. If arrests were made, someone needed to watch the prisoner overnight before their delivery to the House of Correction.

Mary Short was suspected of the crimes, but there was little evidence against her. She and her lodger, Sarah Stevenson, were known troublemakers in the parish, and had threatened to *do for* a number of local residents. In September a local magistrate committed both of them to the sessions at Spilsby for breaches of the peace and they were confined in the House of Correction at Louth. In February, Stephenson, whilst still a prisoner, made a statement to magistrates in which she admitted being present when Short committed a number of offences, or boasted of other criminal acts.

If we are to believe what she said, Short was intent on doing mischief to the family. Stephenson claimed to have been present on a number of occasions when Short released Richardson's sheep onto the highway, stoned the windows of his house and stole clothing, uprooted his vegetables and damaged his fruit trees. She claimed that a parish constable, who searched her house for stolen clothing, helped Mary Short burn them when they were found, as he owed her money. Short boasted of setting fire to one of Richardson's hovels (field barns) in which he stored ploughs and harrows. Stephenson had seen Short when she returned home that night. She had taken a tinderbox, flint, steel and candles with her but had forgotten the matches. Before setting out once more she placed burning sods from the hearth in a pitcher to take with her. Having set the barn alight she stopped only to pull up more of Richardson's potatoes. When she looked back, fire was blazing from the roof of the barn. Short had also killed a dog by tying a brick around its neck and putting it in a poke (a sack), which she had thrown from the river bridge at Coningsby.

Richardson confirmed the loss of, and damage to, his property, and the fire in the barn. Charged and convicted of theft, Short was sentenced to seven years transportation, but it was not carried out. Records show her in Coningsby some years later, still causing trouble.

Christopher Shaw was also to be transported. Suspected of having stolen a greatcoat, the parish constable searched his mother's house and finds him hiding beneath his bed. He denies the theft, but a coat found when the bedcovers are turned back was identified by the owner as his.

Convicted of stealing a muslin apron, Mary Atkin was sent to the house of correction for three months. James Parks, a labourer from Keddington, was the third person that day to be sentenced to transportation after being convicted of stealing two pigs from a farmer at South Willingham. Transportation was a most useful punishment for disposing of troublesome or difficult parishioners. However many such sentences were served out on the prison hulks along the Thames and south coast. That may have been what happened to Mary Short.

Five men charged with riot, assault and forcible entry did not appear.

The bench then fixed the rates for local carriers. The accounts of the County Treasurer, Richard Clitheroe, were examined and approved, and authorisation given for him to raise a further £500 by way of a rate. The coroner's charges for holding eight inquests in the county, and the prison surgeon's costs were settled.

Justices were nominated to oversee the transportation of Mary Short, Christopher Shaw and James Parks. Payments were approved to the dependants of men serving in the Royal Northern Regiment of the Lincolnshire Militia. The Militia Bill for Lindsey amounted to £15 12s 3d to be shared amongst 30 families by the overseers of the parish poor.

At the end of the day the last six prisoners were produced from the stalls below and quickly dealt with by the bench. Sarah Stephenson, so important a witness in the case against Mary Short, was discharged, her purpose served. David Lill who had abandoned his wife to the charge of Holton Holegate parish was similarly dealt with. The other four were all vagrants. Mary Stevens was released to the overseer of the poor at South Somercotes; Rhodia Willett was to spend another three days in the House of Correction before her return on a pass (a warrant) to Asfordby, her last place of settlement; John Roberts was to be whipped next market day along the usual route in the town and kept in the House of Correction for the next sessions, unless, in the meantime, he chose to enrol in His Majesty's sea or land service. John Moody was discharged

Its business uncompleted, the court adjourned to the following morning.

- 6 -

A 'Working System'

THE work of John Howard, and the prison reformers who succeeded him, slowly changed attitudes towards punishment, if not conditions within the gaols. The keeper of the House of Correction in Louth in the 1790s, Thomas Waddington, appears an industrious man well able to cope with change. He was an effective administrator. Apart from his wife, her mother and a watchdog, no mention is made of other assistance in running the prison.

He was not only expected to deliver prisoners to the courts in Louth and Spilsby, but to attend fairs at Horncastle, Brough (Burgh on Baine) and Burwell and liase with local constables to detain vagrants, beggars and wanted persons and return them to Louth. In the event of bad weather, such journeys might entail a night's lodging away and it remains unclear who ran the prison in his absence.

Those 'on the tramp' were ordered by the court to be returned to their last place of settlement after a short spell in the prison, and once again it was the duty of the keeper to deliver them on a warrant, with a copy of their examination, to the next town on their route home.

Some debtors had been removed from the prison system. The folly of detaining them had been recognised, and legislation first restricted their commitment to gaol, and eventually stopped it. The timing was fortunate as it corresponded with difficulties experienced in transporting convicts to 'a place beyond the seas', and made extra capacity available in the prisons for other offenders.

The justices were now more willing to detain convicted felons for up to 12 months, either in the House of Correction at Louth or, more likely, the new bridewell at Kirton. Those convicted of assaults now numbered amongst the felons, and prison may have become a more violent institution. Sentences often carried terms of solitary confinement or hard labour. The two 'solitary' cells at Louth were in the men's yard and their effectiveness doubtful. Whilst desultory attempts had been made at providing work for the inmates, spinning jersey wool or crushing hemp, such activity had not been a priority, and quickly fell by the wayside. There was no 'hard labour'; the inmate's days were idle.

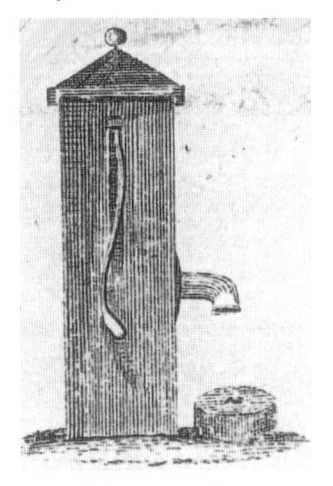

The cost of repair and maintenance remained high. Stone flags in the yards were re-laid, and the gates re-set. The water pump and the well continued to give trouble. A new stable with a loft, and a large shed were constructed in the prison garden. Taxes were paid on a watchdog for the keeper and a heavy draught horse, probably to haul a cart or wagon for the transport of prisoners to and from the courts at Louth and Spilsby. Pigs or hogs were kept by the keeper in the prison grounds to aid in the disposal of unfit food. Two vaults were dug, their purpose unclear, but they may have been intended as punishment cells for recalcitrant prisoners. The purchase of a new mangle, and a charge of two guineas for (?lime) washing the prison every quarter hints at an attempt at cleanliness. The installation of a safe with a lock suggests a secure cabinet for a brace of pistols as had been provided at Kirton. Maybe there were threats of disorder?

Few vagrants left the prison without medical attention or clothing. Susan Cribb and Fanny Cooper with four children between them were eventually returned to Lincoln by Thomas Waddington, but not before they received two weeks medical care, and were provided with bed gowns and cloaks, and shoes for all the family. The water pump failed yet again and was replaced. An oven and grate were installed in one of the low rooms. The front door and some of the fencing round the garden were painted, and when the Reverend Woley Jolland became chaplain a new Bible was purchased for the prisoners.

At the end of January 1804, fire destroyed much of the prison roof. A workman took the blame. A fire left burning in the grate of a chamber where he was working raged out of control when he went for his breakfast. Both Louth fire engines were brought to the blaze. Worked by five men each they helped bring the fire under control. There seems to have been no personal injury, but the subsequent debris took 20 men a day's work to clear. Local churchwardens, and the keepers of the Rising Sun and the White Swan inns provide ale and victuals. It was something of a local event.

Two years later, four of the justices, Thomas Coltman, Charles Burrell Massingberd, G. Langton and Richard Elmhirst, were nominated to report on the state and condition of the House of Correction in Louth, and make recommendations as to its future. The reason for their sudden concern is unclear. The justices knew the prison did not comply with standards set by central government for the segregation of inmates. The fire may have unsettled the justices and the steady increase in the number of inmates threatened security. Escapes from custody were a problem, and one in particular brought embarrassment upon the town. The number of prisoners detained in the House varied, but were normally at their highest around the time of the quarter sessions when there were frequently more than 30 inmates. Men outnumbered women about two to one, but a significant number of children and infants were also detained in the House.

From the *Lincoln, Rutland and Stamford Mercury*, November 1806: *Escaped from the Louth House of Correction on the 17th November instant. James Skinner. About 13 or 14 years of age, 4 feet 4 or 5 inches high; had on a blue jacket and trousers, blue and white striped cotton shirt, a new beaver hat, dark worsted stockings; has short brown hair, a small lump on his left ear, is cut on the top of his head, his right elbow stiff, and his arm small above it, and is a little marked with the small-pox; says that he comes from Scotland, but speaks the Yorkshire dialect. – He is supposed to have run away from a ship, as he was seen at Grimsby about a month ago, and his cloathing all new. Five Guineas Reward.*

The prison was now clearly divided in two parts separated by the keeper's dwelling. Men lived in the ground floor of the old part of the prison. They occupied six small rooms in or around their exercise yard. With a ceiling no more than seven feet high, the justices thought the men's day room *dark, close and extremely offensive*. Their three unheated sleeping wards, lined with oak planks, contained *six miserable beds*. The solitary cells were next to an open cesspit in their yard. Unglazed, iron grate windows allowed a little light and ventilation, with wooden shutters against the wind, the cold and the rain. The floors and ceilings of the rooms above were in such poor condition they afforded easy access to the garret and a way of escape across the roof. These chambers were derelict and no longer used by the prisoners. The men's yard was so insecure the occupants of four adjourning houses in Eastgate were able to converse with the prisoners from their gardens.

Water was brought to the men's yard from the scullery in the keeper's house. A second low room in the keeper's lodging fitted with an oven, racking hooks, gallowbaulk (a rack for hanging hooks), bacon baulks and irons was used as the kitchen. In the pantry there was a meat safe and shelves, a bath and a stove in one of the chambers, shutters and papering, a turn-up bedstead and a cupboard, both with folding doors. In the washhouse was a copper and grate. There were hog sties and troughs in the yard, and a well and a lead pump in the close. In the surrounding garden, were an old stable and an open shed.

The women's day room, at 14 feet square, was about the same size as the one used by the men, but their exercise court was smaller, and they had fewer sleeping wards. They were lodged in the new rooms next to the keeper's house. The window of their night chamber on the first floor was barred and glazed, and overlooked their yard and the prison garden beyond. On the day of the justices visit they noted that one of the women was insane. She slept with the keeper's mother-in-law in an adjourning chamber.

There was no regular system of employment for the inmates and no tools to affect a sentence of hard labour. There were no special provisions for the sick, no baths, and without water in the courts there was no way of keeping clean. The lodging rooms were cold, the inmates forlorn, desperate and abandoned. Not surprisingly the keeper claimed difficulty in maintaining good order. The justices found the presence of a prison so near the centre of town extremely objectionable (they had measured the distance from the court house at 543 yards). The sessions hall could not be warmed in winter. The committee formed the opinion that the prison was by no means sufficiently capacious to contain the numbers usually confined there, and, more importantly, was not secure.

The committee reported the present establishment *(if so it can be called) is so radically bad to be beyond effectual improvement*. When the justices presented their findings before the Easter assize 36 prisoners were confined in the House of Correction at Louth. The committee recommended a new general bridewell and court house be constructed at Horncastle to replace the existing buildings at Louth and Spilsby. Their suggestion was not well received. Finding themselves unable to make a decision, the justices referred the matter to the next court at Spilsby, and then again to Horncastle, but still there was no decision. There was considerable public resistance to the closure of the prison in Louth. The court was quickly presented with a petition bearing several hundred local signatures. The petitioners recognised the prison was too small and in a bad state of repair, and suggested it might be rebuilt, enlarged and improved at infinitely less expense than building a new prison in another town. Were they more concerned at a possible loss of trade? The locals claim that as the daily passage boats now linking the ports of Hull and Grimsby provided easy access for offenders likely to commit their depredations upon the towns and villages of east Lindsey, the need of a deterrent, a prison at Louth, would only increase.

Whilst the magistrates prevaricated, John Stotherd escaped from the courthouse at Spilsby. Joseph Cope, a gentleman attorney, was pursuing Stotherd for debts of £100. Cope eventually resorted to law, and a warrant was issued upon Stotherd's goods. William Harmston, the sheriff's officer, was appointed to execute the warrant when it was received at the Bail of Lincoln. Although only 5 feet 7 or 8 inches tall, Stotherd was stoutly made and had a bold look about him. Balding, with brown eyes and whiskers, he had much the appearance of a horse dealer. Anticipating problems, Harmston contacted the local parish constable, Gervais Richardson. They called upon Stotherd at his lands in Coningsby towards the end of January 1807.

When the Sheriff attempted to execute the warrant and seize Stotherd's goods, he found himself violently assaulted and beaten. His face was bloodied. Stotherd was detained by those present, and charged with assault. He was fortunately able to produce sureties, and was released on bail to appear at the next quarter sessions, but failed to do so. His sureties' recognizances of £50 each were forfeited, and the bench issued a warrant for Stotherd's arrest. He was detained and brought before the mid-summer sessions at Spilsby. His dress of drab coloured cloth coat with coloured buttons, light corduroy breeches, stripped worsted stockings and square toed shoes were not the clothes of a pauper. His fancy red and yellow neckerchief and silk hat, with a binding round the crown, showed he was not a man to be taken lightly. The jury convicted him of the assault. Mindful of the need to support their own officers when carrying out the court's directions, the justices sentenced Stotherd to two years imprisonment in the bridewell at Kirton, the first and last months of the sentence were to be in solitary confinement.

Stotherd had other ideas and made good his escape. By local standards, John Stotherd was a high profile prisoner, sentenced for an assault upon a representative of the King's peace. His flight from custody brought shame and ridicule upon the courts.

The following Easter, the justices give Thomas Waddington, the keeper, ten days notice to quit the house of correction. The justices stated that they intended to re-establish a Working System. When a letter was received from officers of the new Bow Street police in London, that Stotherd had been detained, it was the new keeper who was despatched to collect the prisoner.

Travelling by hired coach with coachman and guards, Richard Cox took less than two days to reach London. He paid a reward of 10 guineas to the constables who made the capture, and returned with the prisoner direct to the bridewell at Kirton. Stotherd failed to learn his lesson, and as late as 1823, when he is 54 years old, is still appearing before the justices for breaches of the peace at Coningsby. Finding it ever more difficult to produce sureties for his future good behaviour he spends more and more time in the county gaol. Richard Cox, the new governor, and previously a sheriff's officer from the Bail of Lincoln, was to receive £100 a year in his new post as the keeper of the House of Correction at Louth.

Plans to build a new prison at Horncastle were abandoned. In the spring, tenements and gardens adjourning the Louth prison belonging to Widow Goodhand and her sons were purchased for £225 to provide more land around the gaol. The old houses were taken down and the brick dressed for re use. The £250 set aside for the piecemeal improvement and enlargement of the House of Correction at Louth did not compare well with the £875 being spent on building and furnishing new accommodation and offices for the judges attending the Lincoln Assize, nor the £1,750 authorised by county justices for work needed at the Castle gaol.

The justices received a letter from Sarah Blythe, matron of the House some 20 years earlier. She wrote: *Gentlemen, After 34 years Service in the House of Correction at last I fear a Common Workhouse will be my fate, except your fostering hand will shield me. At the Age of 74, as I am nearly Blind, and of Course Incapable of any Work and the prayers of my Heart will be ever for your Kindness. Sarah Blythe.* The payment of an annuity or pension to previous employees in such circumstances was not unusual, but in this instance there is no corresponding entry in the accounts.

Work on the prison by local builders Robert Foster and George Smith commenced around the prisoners. The new keeper entered his post with enthusiasm. Day, order and labour books, a dictionary and volumes for the justices, quill pens and paper and another Bible were purchased. There was a wainscot desk and stool for Richard Cox, and two assistants were employed to help on sessions days and at busier times in the prison. For the prisoners there were iron pots and pans and a tin saucepan; wooden spoons, plates and dishes; scales, weights and standards; extra coals for cooking their food; five new bedsteads and tin night buckets for the sleeping rooms; a large cinder shovel and a coal scuttle, and 'houldfasts' for the iron fire grates; handcuffs and leg shackles and 'oyle' for the locks. A new well is sunk in the prison yard and a pump fixed. £30 was made available to purchase old rope, and an axe to cut it with, for the men to tease into oakum, and a wheel and wool cards for the women to spin flax.

From the *Lincoln, Rutland and Stamford Mercury,* 11th August 1809: *On Thursday last was committed to the House of Correction at Louth (by the Reverend John Fretwell, Clerk), Elizabeth Penson and Agnes Holderness for deserting their service without leave – and on Friday last David Harrison of Great Steeping (by Reverend George Street) for not performing his work in husbandry. Each for one month's imprisonment.* Here was an example of the House of Correction being used to support the authority of master over servant.

By the close of 1810, the justices were confident that the prisoners could now be divided into four classes. The men and women's sections were subdivided again into those detained for minor offences, misdemeanours and debt, and felons, including prisoners convicted of assaults, and vagrants. Each has a separate courtyard, day room and sleeping wards.

Prison ordnance
A new blunderbuss, powder, shot and fetters
**Lindsey Quarter Sessions A/1/360/95
Lincolnshire Archives Office**

    The governor (the keeper) was to see every prisoner on admission. They were not to be assigned a ward till they and their clothing was clean. To reinforce this move, 36 pounds of soap and four hand towels are purchased every quarter, and Christopher Leake, a local stonemason, fixed stone water troughs and basins in the yards. The prisoners were not fed in the mornings until they had washed and cleaned themselves. New brushes, mops and brooms provided every three months enabled the inmates to sweep the prison daily, and wash through weekly.

    With the exception of those deemed by the surgeon as sick, and housed in two attic rooms, prisoners were released from their sleeping wards at half past six in the morning, not to return until eight o'clock at night. In winter they rose half and hour after sunrise, returning half an hour after sunset. All wards were locked at night. Only the sick rooms in the attic were lit with candles. Where possible inmates slept on wooden bedsteads covered with *stout bedrugs and blankets* purchased locally from Eve and Campbell (now Eve and Ranshaw). Vagrants detained for less than a week were kept separate from other prisoners (surely a fifth class) and allowed loose straw on the Yorkshire stone flagging instead of the common bedding of the prison.

Visits to debtors could take place whenever they were not working. Those calling upon other prisoners were liable to be searched, and friends of those convicted of an offence were only allowed 15 minutes in the presence of the governor.

The chaplain, Rev. Daniel Benson, preached and read prayers to the prisoners every Sunday in a room in the gaoler's house, in theory the only time the different classes of prisoner might see each other. He visited the sick, and spoke to any of the inmates whom he thought his advice and conversation may be of use.

Work continued around the inmates. In January 1811 after the Epithany Sessions, most of the 11 persons remaining in the House were destitute. They awaited their discharge or return to their last place of settlement. John Jacklin, who was dumb, had been unable to find securities to ensure he kept the peace after a disturbance in Goulceby. Another dumb man, Philip Batchelor, had been in the House of Correction since the beginning of November 1810 awaiting his return to Norfolk. He was destitute, and the keeper has been obliged to provide him with shoes and stockings, breeches and a coat. One of the women, Lucy Rawson, was heavily pregnant, and Elizabeth Parker had a child with her.

By the end of February the numbers are beginning to increase. Lidia White and her child, and Elizabeth Davinson were admitted the same day. Elizabeth Davinson was barely covered in rags, and was desperately ill. They were joined by Adam and Margaret Brackenridge, their daughter Eleanor and infant son John. Both father and son were unwell, and the apothecary or surgeon visited almost daily. Wine and brandy were prescribed, a bad sign. Richard Cox was obliged to employ two local women to nurse the sick in an attic room by candlelight. Elizabeth Parker's child fell ill.

At the end of the month Sarah Ogden 'a vagrant', was brought to the house by the constable from Kirkby on Bain. She was to be returned to her last place of settlement, but not before she had been provided with a shift, a gown and apron, stockings and a handkerchief.

When Elizabeth Davinson died at the beginning of March, she had been in the house less than two weeks. She was 25 years old. Despite the efforts of the surgeon and the care of the nurses, the infant John Brackenridge died a fortnight later, and his father at the beginning of April. The coroner, William King, who was also the surgeon, and his jury, found a verdict of *visitation by God* in all three cases. The keeper provided a 'crape' (a shroud), coffins were supplied by Robert Foster, the builder, whose men probably acted as bearers, and the fees of the Church for a burial were paid from funds of the county rate.

Charlotte Astley, a widow, and her daughter Elizabeth were brought to the prison from Fulletby. Lucy Rawson's recovery from the birth of her child was not going well. More vagrants were admitted - John Miller and John Cox, and Sarah Panton and Hannah Jackson. Slowly the numbers rise as the next quarter session nears.

Elsewhere in the county little had changed – the yard at Spalding bridewell remains insecure. Stamford was *offensive and unhealthy*, in Old Shop Lane at Grantham *the whole prison was very dirty*; and at Grimsby where the mayor and justices of the borough claimed to feed the prisoners two pounds of meat a week each, there had been little improvement. In Lincoln the gaoler had opened a quarry in the area of the castle yard, and some of the prisoners worked at raising stone. A New Drop was ordered to be erected on the roof of the Cobb hall in place of the gallows, and the Stonebow Gate jail remained a disgrace to the city.

The dietary, now cooked by the keeper and his wife, the matron, was based around *good household bread*, potatoes, and oatmeal gruel, beef - served in stews and broths, barley puddings and milk. Richard Cox was now allowed 8d a day for every inmate, a shilling for those who were sick. Prisoners engaged in heavy work, and conducting themselves to the satisfaction of the gaoler, were granted a further allowance of *beef sufficient to enable them to perform their labours* - and maintain their weight. Persons sentenced to less than four weeks detention were often given a reduced dietary.

There was yet no prison uniform, but where absolutely necessary clothing was supplied *sufficient to keep them healthy and clean*. Old clothing, boots and shoes were bought in for the vagrants.

The new bridewell at Kirton was the only prison in the county where serious attempts were made to provide for the convicts' labour. Yards and workrooms were furnished with looms; twist mills, hemp-blocks and spinning machines for the inmates' labour. The value of their labour proved so high that the magistrates reduced the proportion the prisoner was able to retain from a half to a third. Perhaps this explains the findings of James Neild when he recorded *I could not help remarking that though the store room was filled with wool, none of the prisoners was at work upon it.*

In 1812 two new punishment or solitary cells were sunk into one end of the debtors' yard at Louth, reached down a short flight of steps. Both cells measured about nine feet by five feet six inches, with access to even smaller enclosed yards; in the corner of each yard was a privy. Robustly built, the brick walls of the cells arched into the ceiling, the iron doors were faced with timber. Escape was unlikely. Without windows and sunlight, and probably painted black inside, the cells were damp, dark and slimy. There was no air revive the foetid corners. They were quite unsuited to habitation.

Confinement in the solitary cells as a punishment for recalcitrant behaviour might be combined with a bread and water diet, the use of irons or trammels, riveted on and removed by the local smithy, (the shackles at Louth weighed six pounds); or whipping with a scourge.

The rooms above the punishment cells were the night wards for debtors and misdemeanants. The garret storey of the extension served as a simple prison chapel, with bench pews for the men and women separated by a pulpit and reading desk for the chaplain and a stall for the matron and keeper. About 70 inmates might attend Sunday prayers.

From the *Lincoln, Rutland and Stamford Mercury*, 11 December 1812: *Committed to the House of Correction at Louth on the 2nd instant by the Reverend William Chaplin and the Reverend M Allington, Pamela Stones for one year's confinement, she having been delivered of a male bastard child chargeable to the Parish of Tathwell.*

When the old town hall was pulled down the justices order the clock to be saved and remounted over the prison. An attic room facing Ramsgate was adapted as the clock chamber, and the old mechanism was cleaned and repaired. The bell was installed on an iron frame in the roof. A new dial was purchased for £2 2s 0d and let into the wall. People living in the east end of town might then know the time.

At night the prison was lit with 'candels', and two oil 'Lantherns' were purchased for the keeper.

In refurbishing and extending the House of Correction the magistrates had extracted the greatest possible accommodation from the available space. There were still no sick rooms, workrooms, visiting rooms or reception rooms. A wooden tub purchased by the keeper was the only means to bathe, and his small kitchen was the only place to cook the food. On completion they employed a third member of staff, a turnkey, to assist the keeper and his wife, at a salary of £10 a year.

Enclosed behind a brick wall eight to ten feet high, the prisoners' quarters consisted of four dayrooms (one for each class) and 17 night cells. All the first floor and most of the attic storey were given over to the sleeping wards. Only the felons spent their nights on the ground floor.

The women's block was only two floors high. The keeper's house next door had an attic, but the roof may not have been raised to provide a third floor as with the rest of the prison. Some of the attic is used for storage.

Water came from the well. When they dug out the privies in the surrounding yards, as they did every three months, the stench was appalling.

From the *Lincoln, Rutland and Stamford Mercury*, July 1816: *On Sunday last the new Chapel at the House of Correction at Louth was opened, and an excellent discourse, suitable to the occasion, was delivered by the Reverend John Loft, Curate of Louth, who took his text from Exodus, chapter 20, verse 8 – 'Remember the Sabbath Day to keep it holy'.*

The Church singers attended and sang several appropriate Anthems.

Louth House of Correction was now the busiest prison in Lincolnshire. Sleeping two to a bed it was judged to have room for a hundred prisoners, 70 men and 30 women, less than a square yard each in the day rooms. As the time for the quarter sessions approached, even the smallest sleeping cell (12 feet by 6 feet) might hold four inmates at night.

A disorganized and wretched place.

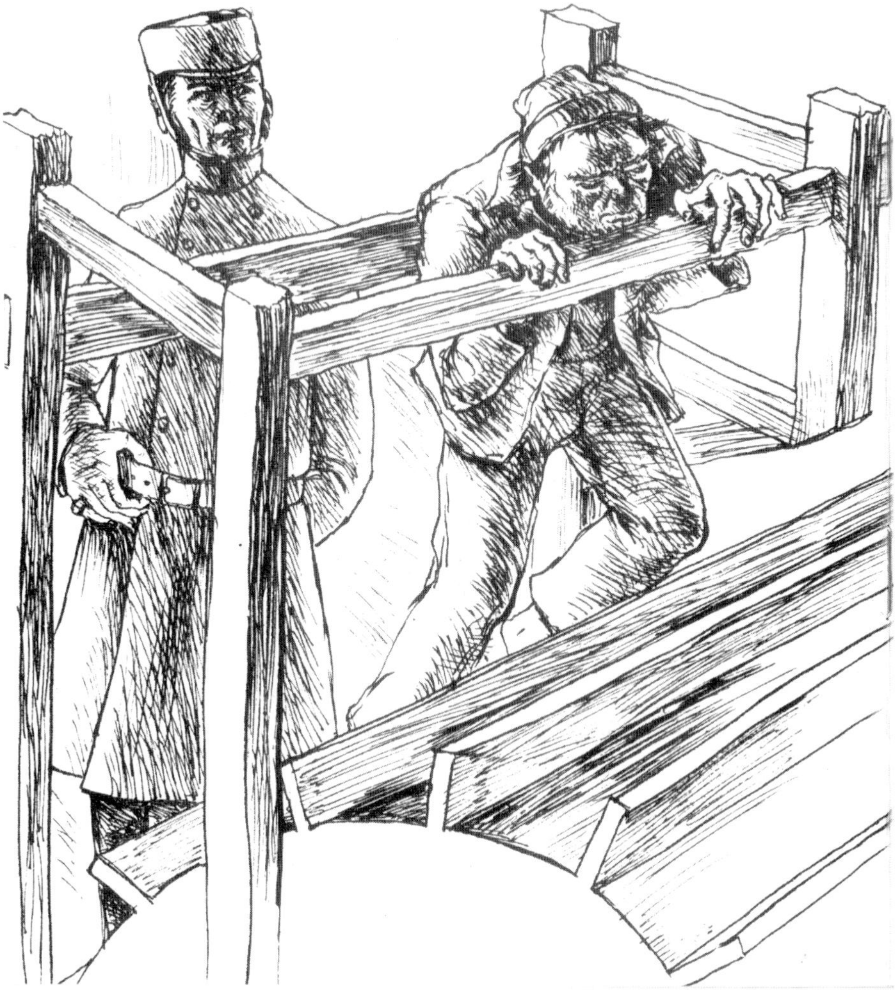

- 7 -

Hard Labour

THE movement for the reform of the Parliamentary system was stifled in 1793 by the outbreak of war with France. To finance the conflict, William Pitt the younger was obliged to raise a tax on income. The price of bread, already high as a result of failed harvests in 1795 and 1796, was further affected by the impossibility of importing grain from Europe. Unemployment and poverty amongst the rural population was a serious problem.

When the Napoleonic Wars came to an end in 1815, new Corn Laws, passed by a Parliament whose members were landowners and farmers, confounded the imports of foreign grain, and kept the price of corn high. Soldiers and sailors returning from arms joined farm labourers seeking work in the towns.

Reduced by unemployment to poverty, and lacking representation both locally and in Parliament, many of the poor took their anger onto the streets. There was violent protest and damage to property.

In Lincolnshire much of the venom was directed against itinerant workers, still important to the farmers at harvest time. Two mounted troup of the North Lincolnshire Militia, more than seventy men, under Captains George Chaplain and William Walker, were despatched to Bardney in response to a request by the local magistrate, the Reverend Thomas Roe, to suppress civil unrest. Over three days of violence, 39 of the rioters were arrested, and several later committed to await their trial at sessions. At Carrington, George Daniel, and Thomas Kirk (alias 'Great Jack'), the ringleaders of a riotous and tumultuous crowd, spread terror amongst the people in an attempt to drive Irishmen from their work on the Fens. Detained and brought to court, they were sentenced to 12 months in the bridewell at Kirton.

Farming drifted into depression and agricultural wages fell.

The first censuses in 1801 and 1811 indicate an acceptance by government that it was responsible for more than raising taxes and a navy. There were inequalities of representation, where old boroughs - the 'rotten' boroughs - returned two members of parliament for few voters, whilst people living in the industrial centres had none. Perhaps fear of civil unrest prompted a review of the prisons.

Central government's account of the gaols, houses of correction and penitentiaries of England and Wales in 1818 recorded 11 such institutions in the county of Lincoln. Lincoln Castle housed the assize prisoners and debtors; the common gaol at Spalding and the house of correction at Kirton and Skirbeck provided custody for the courts of the Parts of Holland. Kesteven used the house of correction at Falkingham, and Lindsey the bridewells at Kirton and Louth. Boston, Grantham, Grimsby, Stamford and the city of Lincoln continued to use their common gaols. Only the prison at Lincoln Castle, where nearly half the inmates were debtors, and the new bridewell at Kirton came near to the capacity of the House of Correction at Louth.

This is not to say that the prison at Louth was physically large. The site in Ramsgate measured little more than 100 feet (35 metres) square, far less than an acre of land. From this area must be deducted the four exercise courts, the prison garden and the keeper's lodgings. The 'T' shaped, two-storied building the prisoners occupied was about 90 feet (30 metres) by 55 feet (20 metres).

At that time the House of Correction was mainly used for convicts sentenced to short spells of 'hard labour', those committed by the magistrates for misdemeanours and vagrancy, and prisoners awaiting trial. There were usually a few local debtors. The gaol calendars show most convicted felons (usually thieves) sentenced by the justices to terms of imprisonment of more than six months as serving their time in the 'new' bridewell at Kirton.

In October that year (1818) the names of 90 inmates were recorded on the gaoler's calendar. One third were female, one in six were children. One wonders how the keeper separated them neatly into four classes. A second turnkey had been recruited.

The judiciary had already dealt with 13 of the occupants. Five debtors in the prison sentenced by the Courts of Requests at Horncastle, Alford and Louth, were being detained for terms of up to 100 days; eight others were serving sentences. Four men had refused to obey the conditions of an affiliation order to maintain their illegitimate offspring, and another was unable to find a surety. Sarah Atkins had abandoned her child upon the parish of Alford, Elizabeth Marshall had run away from service and was to be detained in the House of Correction for one month, and William Steel was serving a sentence of three months for hawking goods without a licence. Everybody else awaited an appearance at the autumn sessions, when the justices took several days to hear all the cases.

The jury convicted all seven prisoners charged with offences. Thomas Rodnam, aged 20, had stolen a side of pork at East Kirkby, and Francis Willoughton, 45, had stolen five or six pecks of wheat. Both were sentenced to seven years transportation. Joshua Johnson was to be detained in the bridewell at Kirton for 12 months for stealing wool, the same fate as Joseph Bradley convicted of an assault. Both men were to spend some time in solitary confinement. It seems that John Stotherd had been causing problems again at Coningsby, being unable to produce sureties to ensure he kept the peace; he was returned to the House of Correction until the next sessions. For causing a disturbance at North Somercotes, 21-year old William Dobson was fined a shilling and sent to the bridewell at Kirton for three months.

The remaining 70 people brought to court from the gaol that sessions appeared under the general description as 'vagrants'. The term vagrant was applied to anybody dealt with under the Vagrancy Acts. An otherwise respectable man who had abandoned his wife and family to the parish rate would be brought before the court as an idle and disorderly person to be dealt with as 'a vagrant'. Similar action would be taken against anybody found other than at their normal place of abode and either unable to support themselves or account for their behaviour. Reduced to begging for food to survive, they quickly came to the notice of parish officers and were brought before the local magistrate. Inevitably convicted of 'vagrancy', they were committed to the House of Correction, most to await their sentence at the next quarter sessions.

In providing for these people, the House was fulfilling its role under the Poor Laws. For the destitute poor, the House of Correction was a place of last resort. They slept rough in barns and outhouses, their clothing insufficient to keep them warm and dry in winter, and survived on frozen turnips hacked from the fields. For many the House of Correction may have seemed an attractive option. Having surrendered to the parish officer, the magistrate had nowhere else for them to be taken. The parish poor houses, and in towns, the houses of industry, were intended for the local paupers. The stranger was brought to the bridewell. Punished for being poor, here at least there was food and clothing, medical attention, shelter and somewhere to sleep. For some there was help in returning home, while others needed encouragement.

When brought before the magistrates' they might be dealt with in a number of ways. Persistent offenders, the incorrigible rogues and vagabonds were committed to a higher court for punishment. For most detained at Louth, there were four alternatives.

Older men, and some of the women travelling with children, were ordered to be returned by the gaoler as soon as possible to their last place of settlement. The distances they travelled, and the expense of returning them was considerable. Seventeen of the inmates were dealt with in this way. Mary Rhodes and her infant daughter Catherine were from Hythe in Kent. Margaret Downley and her children, Louise and Charles, were returned to Ireland through the port of Liverpool, and John Gordon was sent back to Falmouth in Cornwall. Why and how these travellers had journeyed so far is not divulged, nor do we learn of the whereabouts of husbands and fathers. Perhaps the women had been deserted.

Men below the age of 30 were likewise sent back to their last place of settlement, but not before being whipped. The punishment took place at the town market about a fortnight later. Thirteen prisoners are to be whipped over two days. The 20 to 30 lashes administered to each considered severe. The scourge comprised nine lengths of double-knotted whipcord. It was necessary to pay for the attendance of local constables, and a public display of this nature may no longer have met with general approval. Amongst those to be made an example of was Patrick McConner, a man travelling with his wife and two children. The youngest to be thrashed, Richard Harris, was 13 years old.

Fifteen casuals were discharged immediately. The courts might take this action if it was unlikely a 'place of settlement' could be resolved, or the prisoner was able to convince the magistrates they were genuine travellers with a destination in mind. Passes were issued to facilitate such a journey, asking the bearer be given all reasonable assistance. Two older men in this group had their children with them, but most were under 20 years old. The names of some of them, - John Dubois, Dominik Waka, Augustine Negro and Anthony Guffor indicate they may have been of foreign extraction.

The remaining 21 prisoners, including most of the women with children, were returned to the house of correction to await a decision at the Epithany sessions.

When the keeper took them to Spilsby on the 15th January, four were ordered to be returned home, and the rest were simply discharged. Fifty six other prisoners were carted from the prison to be dealt with before the court.

With the prison stuffed full with beds, there can be little surprise that the entry for Louth in the government survey records there is no room for working. This was an understatement to say the least, and an omission the justices intended to address.

The prison system was changing. The ideas of John Howard and the reformers compromised a punitive judiciary. Improvements to the sanitary arrangements and greater attention to cleanliness reduced outbreaks of disease and the gaol fever. Men and women were separated. The supply of spirituous liquors, the payment of fees and garnish slowly came under control. The first of the penitentiaries, allowed for by the Prison Act of 1791, opened at Millbank in 1816, but had not been a success. There were several new local prisons; they were part of a penal system, but without employment for the inmates, the habit of industry was lost. Offenders were returned to society more dissolute than ever.

Extracts from the Prison Rules 1821

Chaplain to read prayers and preach every Sunday.

Chaplain to read the rules every quarter in the presence of the prisoners.

Every prisoner to be examined by the surgeon, and not passed to the appointed ward till clean. Females to be examined in the presence of the Governor's wife.

No dogs, pigs or poultry except the Governor's Watchdog.

Governor shall have no lodgers.

No gaming allowed.

No spirituous liquor unless on the order of the surgeon.

No excuse for exemption from work other than by surgeon's report.

No prisoner to receive his food till he has cleaned himself.

No linen or clothes brought for the use of prisoners shall be received unless they are clean.

Visitors to be searched if suspected of concealing anything.

Vagrants committed for seven days or less to sleep on straw instead of the common bed.

Wards to be whitewashed twice a year.

Prisoners set to work shall receive half their earnings on discharge.

Prisoners refusing to work shall be kept on bread and water.

Governor to have the power to fetter prisoners on capital charges or acting in a refractory manner, providing the Visiting Magistrates are informed.

Any prisoner refusing to obey the rules, acting in an indecent manner, damaging prison property or attempting to escape shall be considered an offender.

The Governor may support offenders on a bread and water diet, and place them in close confinement provided Visiting Magistrates are informed and allow continuance of the punishment.

Rules and Regulations for the Louth House of Correction
Agreed at the Spilsby Epiphany Sessions in 1821 to mark the final development of the old house of correction. Staff and justices were unaware of the existence of these rules, or an earlier set of regulations from 1809, when a prison inspector called at a later date, a measure perhaps of their importance to the way in which the prison functioned.
Lindsey Quarter Sessions

William Cubitt's treadmill resolved the problem of setting the inmates to work of a punitive nature, and it was hoped would cure them of their idle ways. Developed in 1818 to provide employment for the inmates of the gaol at Bury St. Edmunds, its use was quickly seized upon by those responsible for other prisons.

Prisoners walked steps around the outside of a metal cylinder, where their weight turned the drum and its axle and provided a source of power. The mills were adapted to pump water, grind and dress corn, beat hemp or crush oats and beans. Where there was no obvious use for the prisoners' labour, the wheels ran against a friction lever, a flywheel or hydraulic regulator; they ground the wind, the operator's effort was wasted.

The wheels varied in length according to local circumstances. The longest at Coldbath Fields in London had eight sections worked by 30 men apiece. Most mills were smaller, with places for between four and a hundred prisoners. The diameter of the wheel, the speed at which it ran and its resistance, the height of the steps, the age and fitness of the offender and the time spent by each prisoner on the wheel, all contributed to the effect of a most chastening experience. With no common design, there was considerable variation in the labour extracted from those ordered to work the treadmill.

In May 1820, Thomas Saunderson, a local stonemason, William Hurst, bricklayer, and Robert Foster, joiner were contracted by the justices to commence work on a walking mill for the House of Correction at Louth. Built beyond the prison gates in Watery Lane (Eastgate) the mill, and a small lodge, formed the southern boundary of the prison yard. The simple two-storey building was divided in two sections.

The lodge on the corner of Ramsgate was a dwelling for the turnkeys. Each had a living room with a fireplace, and a bedchamber above reached by a shared stairway. They overlooked the entrance where new brickwork arched over a pair of fine oak gates nearly eight feet high.

Behind the turnkeys' lodge the remainder of the building housed the treadwheels and the mill, with access was from the prison yard. The two working rooms were separated by a workshop where the power from the wheels was geared to the millstones on the floor above. Eighteen feet long and six feet in diameter, the wheels were slightly larger than most, and filled the length of the room. The 24 wooden stepping boards on the circumference of the wheel were two and a half inches thick and nine inches high. With 12 men working the boards it was important that the working rooms were well ventilated. The wheels gave meaning to a sentence of 'hard labour'

Prisoners faced the wheel in their own bay, and by holding onto a supporting bar, climbed the steps on the outside. After 30 rounds of

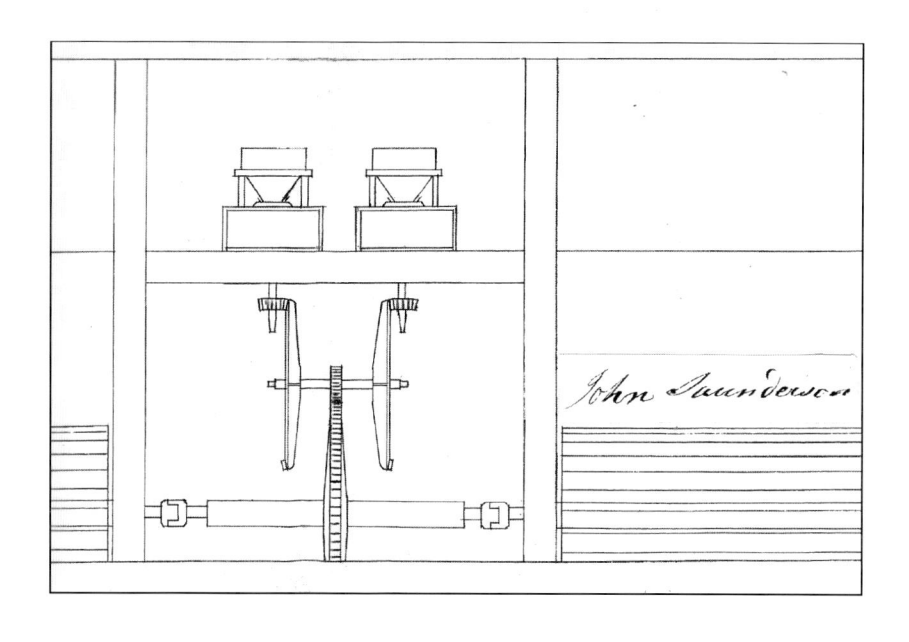

Treadwheel
From John Saunderson's fairly basic 'plan'
The driven mill stones are on the floor above.
Lindsey Quarter Sessions B/5/Louth Box 1. 1820
Lincolnshire Archives Office

Prisoners at work in the Treadmill
Louth Local Study Topics No. 4: The Prison
Louth Teachers' Centre

the wheel they rested for 15 to 20 minutes, their place being taken by another prisoner. The wheel at Louth normally turned at 48 steps a minute, but could reach nearly double this speed. The miller, on the floor above, regulated the rate at which the mill turned, by the speed at which he fed grain to the revolving stones. The rooms on either side of the stones were used as granaries, the windows netted against the entry of birds. The mill is not considered secure, and the men were watched by one of the turnkeys.

In eight hours a prisoner on the Louth mill climbed 8,650 feet. The Society for the Improvement of Prison Discipline recommended 10,000 feet as a minimum. At Durham it was nearly half as much again. The wheel turned for 10 hours in the summer, reducing as the days shortened to about seven hours in the winter.

Only the aged and infirm are not set to the wheel. Unconvicted prisoners were allowed to walk the wheel if they wished. At Louth, women did not walk the wheel, but made and repaired, and washed the clothing and bedding of the prison. Calico and flannel purchased locally from Eve and Campbell, together with buttons, needles and tapes were made up into garments by the women who also stitched and sewed boots and shoes from leather, best thread, wax and nails bought in for the purpose. Inmates needed the garments and footwear they produced. Work as a washerwoman was dirty, wet and often cold. Doubtless the prison used a dolly tub, but struggling with wet, heavy materials used in bedding and attire was as tiring and relentless as the wheel,

Richard Cox, the keeper, is pleased with the wheel. He states he is: *confident the health of the prisoners is improved by the labour of the treadmill, and their conduct since they have been thus employed, has been more orderly than before. The morals of the prisoners when employed are much better than when in idleness. In the latter case they were frequently inventing some mischief, gaming, quarrelling with each other, or using profane and debauched conversation; but now they are employed and under inspection, their behaviour is good and orderly, and they pay increased attention to the religious instruction of the chaplain.*

The keeper's wife sold the flour from the mill at the prison gate. The poor bought most of the milled grain at tuppence a stone under the market price. Receipts, pitifully small, were set against the cost of running the jail. Prisoners walking the mill were paid a penny a day, collected on discharge.

Operation of the mill involved further expense. They needed corn and meal shovels, 'sives' and scuttles, shrouds about the gears, measurers and gauges, 'rowlers' and a weighing machine, brass and small iron weights, sack tackle and 'roap', a step ladder, sail cloth, picks, pales, brushes and oil. Whitewash brushes and cans, lime and turpentine, 'boild' oil, and varnish to smarten the woodwork were also

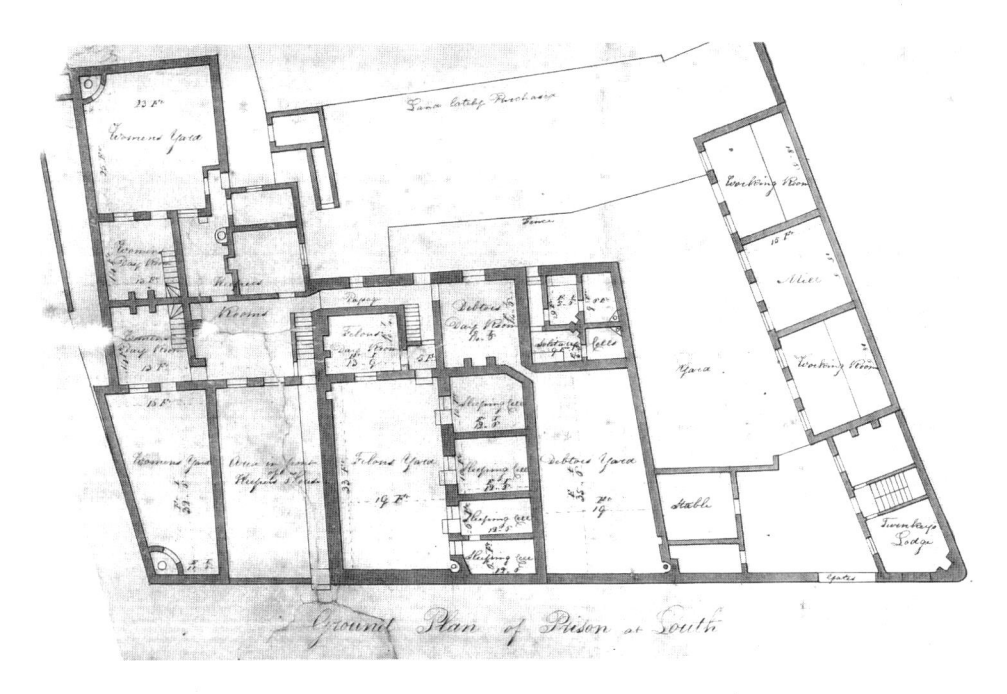

Louth Prison, 1820
The final development of the old house of correction. The working rooms house the treadwheels either side of the mill, with a granary above. The night cells are on the second and attic storeys where there is a small Chapel. The original buildings are in the centre.
Louth Museum Collection

South Elevation of the "Walking Mill" on Eastgate (see page 68)
Lindsey Quarter Sessions B/5 Louth
Lincolnshire Archives Office

purchased. French grind stones needed rounding and replacing, and working machinery required maintenance. A miller, at £12 10s 0d (£12.50p) a quarter became the fourth member of staff, and John Cox was promoted head turnkey.

Books were purchased (from the stationers J & J Jackson in the Market Place) in which to record the prisoners' labour, a Ready Reckoner was needed, wafers (discs of flour and gum to fasten slips of paper together), a binder for copies of Hue and Cry, and Police Gazette, red tape, twine and a map of Lincolnshire, bottles of ink, blotting paper, pens, calendars, Nield's book on prisons, and Phillips on Evidence. The governor needed a post book and sealing wax, forms for weekly diets, copies of the Prison Regulation Act and a Police Dictionary, printed calendars for Louth and Lindsey, and copies of Bramwall and Cresswell's legal reports. The clock needed repairing. A medical journal was also maintained.

Joseph Brackenbury, the aged Clerk of the Peace, acquired a cushion for his chair. For the prisoners there were more blankets and rugs, calico and cotton, hessian and thread, hose and flock. Bibles, prayer books, pewter plates, ash scuttles and coal baskets were purchased. A large table for the debtor's room, a new range in the kitchen, a portable slipper bath and a washtub were provided. Fustian trousers for convicted men signal the first move towards a prison dress; others wear their own clothes.

The refurbishment of the House of Correction and the incorporation of a treadmill proved expensive, and certainly amounted to more than £700. Louth cost nearly as much to operate as the new bridewell at Kirton, both costing the county up to £450 a year. There were other sizeable expenses. Lindsey's contribution towards the Castle prison and the assize court amounted to nearly £900, and the administration of vagrancy orders nearly as much again. Melton's cottages, houses and land adjourning the Louth prison, were purchased for £119 6s10d. There were salaries and expenses for the town clerk, coroner, chaplain, Clerk of the Peace, weights and measurers and corn inspectors, and sundry other matters. The County Treasurer had to raise £3,000 a year as Public Stock to finance the administration.

On 13th February 1821, Mary Chapman was committed to the House of Correction for vagrancy by the magistrate, John Fytche. She had consumption. Another woman, Jane Lingsby, who was in labour, was brought in the same day and Rev. Wolley Jolland, the prison chaplain, baptised her 'base child' William. Both Chapman and Lingsby were amongst those attended by the surgeon. Midwifery (at one guinea), a Bolus (large pills, likely a placebo) and clothes were required for Lingsby and her child. Pearl barley, ointment and 'a mixture' for Chapman, were soon followed by the first of her bottles of wine. The desperate lives of many of the poor led inexorably to the houses of correction where they joined the company of others in like situations. Thrown closely together to suffer 'the itch', with their fevers and gout, asthma and ague and consumption, syphilis and gonorrhoea, worms and scurvy, epilepsy, rheumatism, lumbago and diarrhoea, one can only marvel they survived at all. If the justices were alarmed at the 'effluvia' when prisoners were brought to court, what can the atmosphere have been like in their wards? Unwashed bodies and ragged clothes, the tang of sweat and urine. When Mary Chapman died at the end of April, she is certainly not alone. In this tiny prison, 115 other inmates surround her.

There can be little doubt that all classes of prisoner were hopelessly mixed together. There was disorder, but not anarchy. In a sense the inmates acquiesced in their situation. The keeper, with so few officers, depended upon the co-operation of the prisoners for the House of Correction to function.

The calendar, printed locally by Jacksons, showed the majority of prisoners to be men, with several awaiting trial. The petty theft of flitches of bacon and ham, pecks of potatoes, a sheep's skin, a black guilt pig and sacks of wheat, a gun and six steel traps, reflected the farming nature of the area. More mundane items included a pair of half boots, a waistcoat, a gown and a half handkerchief, and small amounts of cash. Two men required sureties for their good behaviour towards their wives, three others to keep the peace, especially towards the clergy at Tetford, the Rev. Poynt Stewart.

Half the vagrants were less than 30 years old; a dozen of the others were children. Several appeared to be travelling in groups. Nine travellers, the youngest two years old, in the care of two older women were admitted the same day. A small group of debtors, 10 men already convicted of petty larceny and poaching, and the usual collection of young men and women imprisoned in connection with bastardy, the abandonment of such children to the care of parish, and breaches of affiliation made up the rest.

But the gaoler's calendar, the list of prisoners in the gaol at the Easter sessions, does not present the full picture. His accounts for the same quarter, presented to the justices for the payment of the expense of running the prison, record the names of more than sixty other prisoners victualed in the gaol that quarter: 50 men, eight women and two children. Admitted and discharged from the House between one sessions and the next, their names do not appear on the calendar. They had been committed to the prison by a lesser court. Magistrates or justices, sitting without a jury might convict and sentence misdemeanants (minor offenders) with a short term of imprisonment

It is difficult to say when these courts first started, as their early records have not survived. Thomas Dixon, one of the justices of the peace for Louth, recorded fortnightly meetings taking place from June

Lincoln, Lindsey.

THIS is to certify that WILLIAM KING, Coroner, took an Inquisition on the Body of *Ellen Wallace accidentally drowned*

Grainthorpe
April 28th 1821

Witness *John Campion*

Foreman of the Inquest.

Lincoln, Lindsey.

THIS is to certify that WILLIAM KING, Coroner, took an Inquisition on the Body of *Mary Chapman died in Prison of a Consumption*

Louth
April 28th 1821

Witness *Pearson Bellamy*

Foreman of the Inquest.

Coroners certificate
All deaths in the prison were investigated by the coroner and his jury. William King, coroner, was also the prison surgeon
Lindsey Quarter Sessions A/1/457/57
Lincolnshire Archives Office

1792. The justices met in the town hall on a Wednesday from eleven in the morning until two o'clock in the afternoon. His written note probably confirms an informal situation in existence for some time. The George Inns at Alford and Horncastle were being similarly used by 1796. Such courts were not restricted to the towns, but also met in larger parishes where local magistrates lived to resolve minor disputes or instances of disorder, with a room and a fire, food and drinks provided by the keeper of the village inn. Committals by magistrates sitting at the petty sessions accounted for an increasing number of the prison's population.

'Memorials' of convictions at petty sessions ought to have been forwarded by the magistrates to the quarter sessions clerk for noting in the minutes. This was sometimes overlooked. Detention of the additional men in the prison shows regularity. Five were detained overnight (public disorder perhaps), but most remained seven to 10 days, two, four, six and eight weeks. Tuesdays and Saturdays were noticeable days of admission, but there was no regular pattern. Nearly half were admitted and discharged on the same day as another inmate; perhaps as labourers and vagrants they travelled together for safety. A man and his wife were imprisoned for 14 days.

The eight additional women present a slightly different picture. None were admitted in company with another and they seem to have been travelling alone. Jane Lingsby was discharged with her newborn son four weeks after the birth - maybe a 'lying in' process. Margaret Wright and her child remained a little over eight weeks. The remainder were detained either two or four weeks. Elizabeth Chapman is shown on the calendar as a vagrant, but died in the House of Correction a few days before the court sits.

There was a steady turnover of the gaol population in Louth. If the justices were to continue sentencing people so rigorously, they needed more accommodation.

Sketch from the notebook of William Brown (1788-1859)
painter of the Louth Panorama

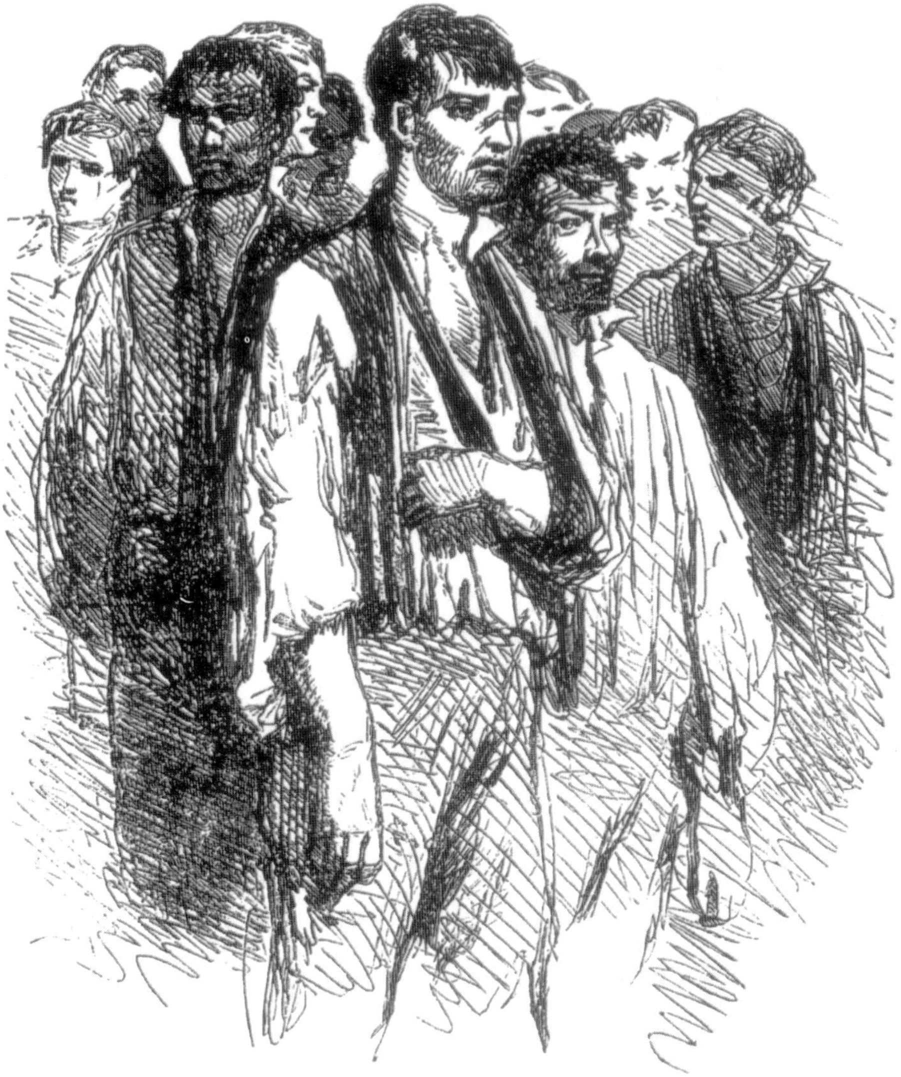

- 8 -

New Eastgate Jail – old problems.

WHEN Robert Foster was asked to draw a plan of the gaol and its tread wheel at the close of 1823, the decision had been taken to build a new prison at Spilsby, and to improve and enlarge the House of Correction in Louth. Whilst this action was not in accordance with the ideas of central government, the justices perceived they had little choice.

The prison building in Louth was a piecemeal development of a simple 17th century lock-up. Whilst it was possible to keep the men and women separate, further classification was only attended to as far as the prison will admit. A shortage of rooms meant occupants slept two to a bed. Without baths, infirmary or reception rooms the prison was quite unable to meet the standards required by Robert Peel's Gaol Act of that year. The transportation of large numbers of prisoners by horse and cart between the quarter sessions at Spilsby and Louth four times a year was also less than satisfactory.

Growing civil unrest gave no cause for the justices to believe that an increase in the number of people committed to the prison within the last 20 years would not continue. In Lincolnshire problems between migrant workers, still needed by the farmers in the autumn to thresh the corn, and the indigent population remained. Vagrancy would not go away. The justices responded to a perceived local need for greater prison accommodation, and had the confidence to vote the funds to deal with the problem.

Henry Edward Kendall was chosen as the architect for both Lindsey prisons. With offices in London he was a man of some reputation. Examples of his work had been exhibited at the Royal Academy. The two prisons were constructed on similar lines. Spilsby, the larger of the two, was to include an infirmary and a new sessions house. Plans were quickly approved, and the chairman of the bench, John Bateman Dashwood, laid the foundation stone the following June.

There were difficulties at Louth. Enlargement of the House of Correction entailed the purchase of more land. Property between the jail and the River Lud, and the prison and Espin's Priory was owned and occupied by a number of town's folk who were reluctant to sell. Six homes need to be purchased.

Fortunately for the justices, one occupant had died and trustees were administering the property. A price was agreed. The Coulam family proved more difficult. Three of the houses were theirs, variously occupied by two sisters, father and son. Visited personally at home, they eventually agreed to give the sale some thought. A paddock and orchards surrounded William Petch Kime's house and garden. He was ill. There were disputes over boundaries, and he insisted on several valuations. Robert and Ann Bywaters failed to respond to letters, and their deeds were not forthcoming. The town's solicitor called on the various owners, taking with him a copy of the Act of Parliament under which the property could be taken by the magistrates. He explained the content and requested them to 'fix a price' to help them make a decision. Orders of Court to purchase the homes were obtained. When the owners set their price it was not challenged, and William Coulam's valuation was later increased by nearly ten per cent.

After eight months work, and legal fees of nearly £200, the land was theirs. Six acres including the old House of Correction, bounded by Eastgate, Ramsgate, the River Lud and the Priory, a site eight times the original.

By the end of August, Kendall had produced working drawings for the project at Louth, effectively a new jail. Advertisements were placed in the Times, the Morning Post and local newspapers inviting tenders for the work. Contracts were signed in November.

Whilst the decision by the justices to build two new prisons may be understood, the debt they were willing to incur in doing so is almost unbelievable. In the light of their previous care in spending public funds on the inmates of the gaol, the likely expense may have been something of a shock. The estimated final cost of the prison at Spilsby, including fitting out was £25,300. The Loan Office of the Exchequer agreed a loan.

For ratepayers already concerned about the rising cost of supporting the poor, such extravagance by their justices, previously so careful of the accounts, may appear scandalous. In addition to financing the new prison, existing commitments bore heavily upon the funds. Alongside its normal operational cost, the bridewell at Kirton needed repair and improvement costing nearly £1,000. There were salaries for the jail staff, the surgeon, the chaplain, and Lindsey prisoners lodged in the King's Bench and Marshalsea prisons. There was maintenance of the county prison at Lincoln, and contributions towards the new county hall and judges residence; expenses to be claimed in the prosecution of felons, and for apprehending and returning vagrants to their place of abode; the repair of county bridges and sundry other claims made upon the finances by the Clerks of the Peace, the magistrates at Tetford and Horncastle, and the town clerk for Louth; prison repairs at Alford, and claims by the coroner, the militia, chief constables, and sheriff's officers; the treasurer's salary, the cost of stamps, and the burial of drowned seamen. A new set of weights and measures in three mahogany boxes cost £145. In total, the parish rate to be collected by the constables of Lindsey in 1826 needed to balance expences approaching £17,000.

In deciding to build the new prisons, the justices were not alone. In the 1780s a number of local jails and bridewells had been refurbished as a result of Howard's work for reform. A second wave followed in the 1820s when the efforts of Elizabeth Fry and the Quakers further improved conditions and treatment in local prisons owned and managed by County and Borough justices. Not surprisingly much importance was attached to reforming the penitent sinner, and the role of the prison chaplain grew in importance.

At the same time central government, driven by growing resistance to transportation and the filthy and overcrowded conditions in the prison hulks, was striving to establish its own network of penitentiaries for convicted prisoners. We are starting to see the development of parallel administrations.

Spilsby prison began admitting prisoners early in 1827. Work at Louth was completed later that year. To the justices, Louth, with its treadmill and greater capacity, remained the favoured prison.

There can be little doubt that the new prison was a striking if not a brooding presence on the edge of town. Built in the middle of the site facing Eastgate, Kendall's design was three storeys high, and dominated the surrounding area. A number of savings were made to the original plan. A mill house and sheds for new treadwheels next to the airing yards were not fitted out, and only two of three planned wings were completed. This helped to reduce the final cost of work at Louth from an estimated £20,000 to an Exchequer loan of £12,000. A spacious keeper's residence at the centre of the prison linked the north and east wings in an 'L' shape. Above the keeper's house was the prison chapel.

Both wings were flagged with stone. On each floor six 'single' sleeping cells (32 in total at Louth, 63 at Spilsby) opened onto a double passage. Each cell measured eight feet by six and was secured by an iron door fitted with a large circular ventilator. Internal walls were a brick and a half thick. High in the outside wall to each cell was a barred window. Each cell had an iron bedstead, a straw mattress, two blankets, a rug and a night tin. As there was no heating an extra blanket was provided in winter. The passage led to the day rooms, which, on the ground floor, give access to eight walled airing yards around the building. The yards provided somewhere to exercise, a

LOUTH - PRISON -

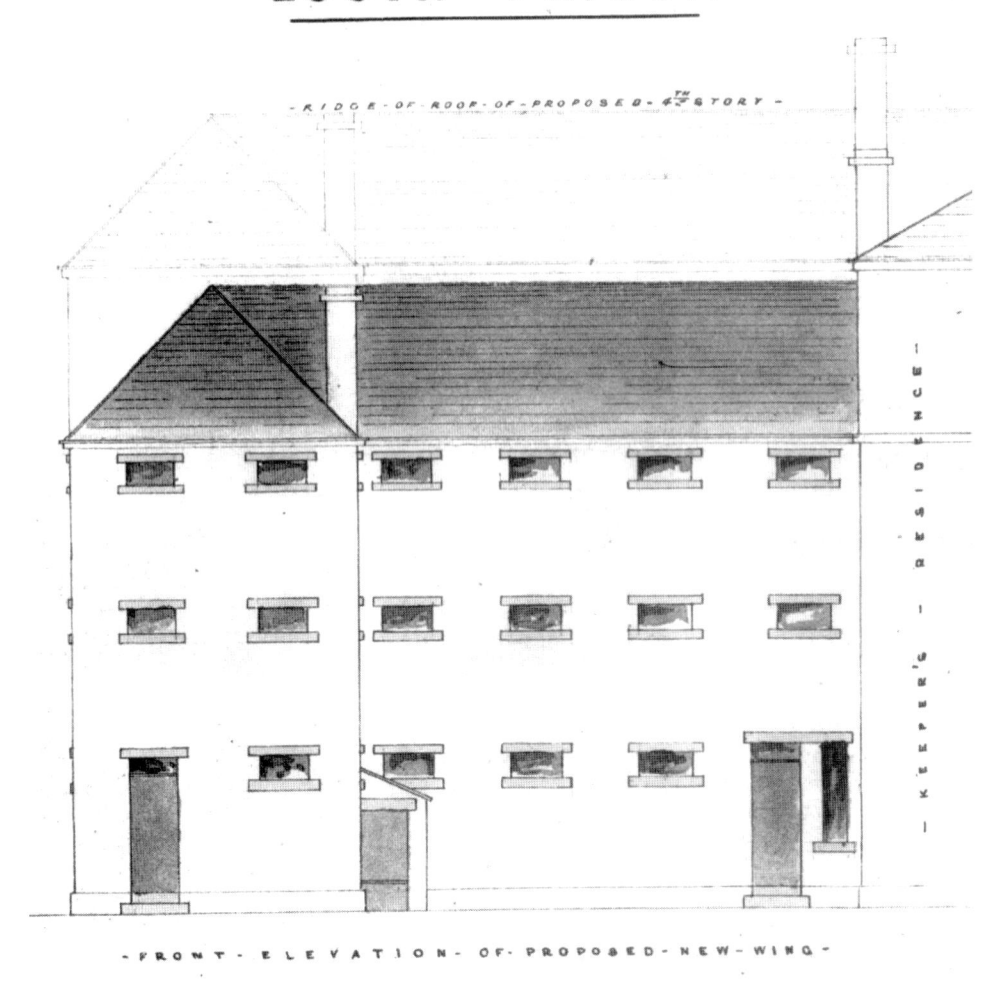

Proposed West Wing from plans prepared by the County Surveyor, J.S. Padley in 1848 when consideration was given to enlarging the new gaol. It was never built, but gives an idea of what the existing cell block looked like.
Lindsey Quarter Sessions B/5/Louth
Lincolnshire Archives Office

privy and washing cisterns for the different classes of prisoner. Less than 15 metres long and six metres wide, these tiny airless yards surrounded by high walls were cold and bleak in winter but served as crucibles in high summer when the affect on the privies in each corner must have been dreadful.

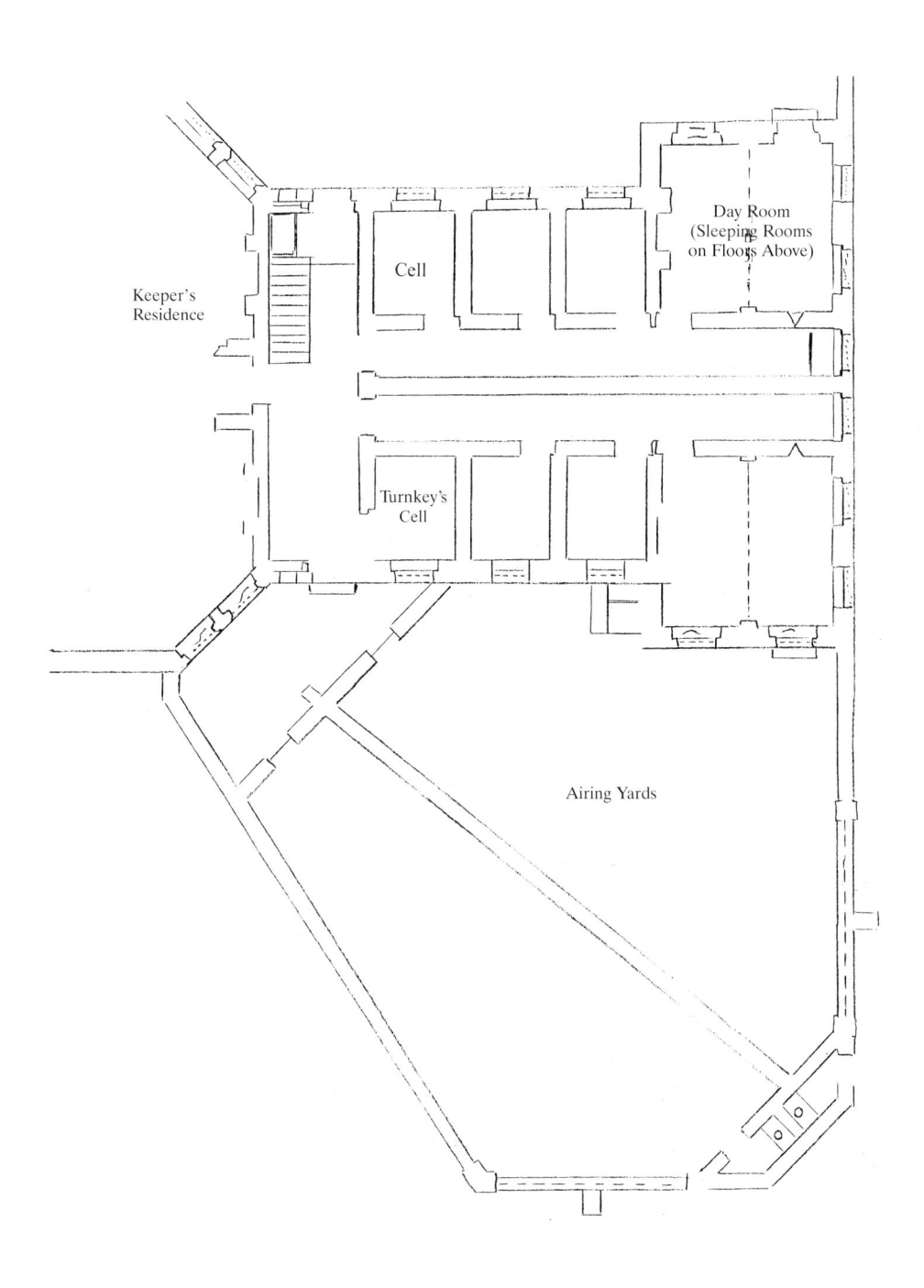

Ground Plan (with airing yards) and elevation
A new wing for Louth Prison, 1824 (completed 1827)
Lindsey Quarter Sessions B/5/Louth
Lincolnshire Archives Office

Extracts from the Spilsby Prison inventory

Prison
63 iron bedsteads
6 double bedsteads
52 straw bed mats
52 straw beds
148 blankets
50 rugs
20 iron benches
3 deal dressers
6 deal tables
18 iron coal boxes
18 iron blowers
18 stone sinks

7 coal baskets
14 dietary boards
63 inventory boards
6 wood pails
113 chamber pots
22 quart cans
59 pint cans
14 pair leg irons
2 brands
Blunderbuss
2 brace of pistols
3 cutlasses

2 rows pegs
11 tin candlesticks
Carpenters tools
Steels yards
Salting vat lined with lead
Forcing pump
Patent weighing machine
Standard scales and seven brass weights

Wash house
Soft water trough
Stone sink
2 copper furnaces

1 brass cock
Washing bench
2 washing stools

7 Washing tubs
4 pair steps
9 stone water troughs

Kitchen
Large table
2 pewter dishes
1 carving knife and fork
1 cleaver
1 chopping block

2 tin ladles
4 gruel cans
1 pestle and motor
Soup can
Cocoa strainer
2 boiling nets

Meat Saw
2 Lanterns
butcher's cratch
Salt Mill

Laundry
Iron store and platform
7 flat irons

3 linen horses
1 clothesline
3 folding boards

Wrangle

Chapel
2 sets fire irons
Pegs and shelves
2 Elin chairs

4 window rollers
2 large prayer books
70 small brasses

2 surplices
Childs crib
Stone sink

Turnkey's Lodge
Copper furnace
Stone sink and brass cock
1 bell
Square deal table

Coffee and teapots
Tin hipbath
Thermometer
Pair of crutches
2 knives and forks

Police lantern and bell
Capping bill
Press bedstead

Governor's House
Oak Penbroke table
Floor carpet
Rolls of matting
Double Oak chest Coat horse

Large deal bookcase with drawers and nests
1 armchair and 3 single chairs

12 mahogany chairs
Wine cellar
6 bells
15 pair of handcuffs

Lindsey Quarter Sessions records B5/Spilsby 1824-25
Lincolnshire Archives Office

The boundary wall 18 feet high and topped with courses of loose brick enclosed the gaol between Eastgate and Ramsgate. The land beyond the wall, towards the river and Espin's Priory, was the prison garden with cowsheds, a stable, pigsties and fruit trees.

Open space between the keeper's house and the entrance in Eastgate was seeded with grass and clover. The ornamental Doric gateway in the perimeter wall was flanked on either side by two lodges, one for the turnkey and the other a laundry and washhouse. The word 'PRISON' was carved in stone above the entrance in large letters.

In the southwest angle of the prison wall remained an old and dilapidated building - the former house of correction.

It is difficult to understand why the justices accepted Kendall's design. The new building lacked its own kitchen, sick room or infirmary. There was no place for a surgeon's examination on admission, or baths for the inmates' cleanliness. These were all omissions, known only too well to the justices, for their absence at the old house of correction. The day rooms were remote from the turnkey's office, and the occupants unsupervised. The absence of rooms where the prisoners might receive useful instruction in reading and writing was a clear breach of the Gaol Act.

Not all prisoners at Louth were transferred to the new building. The old house of correction remained in use for those detained under the vagrancy laws where they were locked up alone at night without officers.

The keeper's substantial residence controlled entrance up the steps into the new prison. The cellars, office and kitchen were essential for the reception and administration of the new works. Green Pickling blinds on brass rods shielded the barred windows, and red oilcloth covered the floors and passageways. For the five officers of the prison there were desks and bell pulls, writing tables and mahogany stools. A bookcase, and cupboards with locking doors lined the walls.

The principal turnkey dealt with new admissions. Convicted felons were stripped and searched on admission and dressed in prison clothes. They were readily identified by their fustian (coarse cloth made of cotton and flax) jacket or smock, and blue trousers. Misdemeanants were clad in fustian suits, but all others, including the women, wore their own clothes. Since many of the poor committed to the prison were dressed in rags, the purchase of second-hand clothes, boots and shoes for men, women and children remained one of the keeper's essential expenses. Without a wash, bath or medical examination, committals were taken direct to the cells in the new prison or one of the tiny wards in the old building.

In the summer, prisoners were unlocked at six in the morning. Night buckets were emptied and candles provided to light the stove in the day rooms. At half past six, the miller escorted the prisoners, one room at

Prisoners confined for various Offences.

#	Name	Offence / Sentence	Magistrates
1	Mildred Clarke,	Committed the 15th day of December, 1824, for having had a Bastard Child chargeable to the parish of Grimoldby. Ordered to be imprisoned and kept to hard labour Twelve Calendar Months.	George Chaplin and John Fytche, Esqrs.
2	John Moss,	Committed the 18th day of May, 1825, for want of Sureties in Bastardy.	John Fytche, Esq.
3	John Davison,	Convicted of Poaching the 22nd day of June, 1825. Ordered to be imprisoned Three Months, unless the sum of Five Pounds Penalty be sooner paid, and to stand committed for Three Months longer, unless a further Penalty of Ten Pounds be sooner paid.	Rev. J. Mounsey
4	Frances Broddell,	Committed the 6th day of July 1825, for having had a Bastard Child chargeable to the parish of Great Carlton. Ordered to be imprisoned and kept to hard labour Twelve Calendar Months.	John Fytche, Esq. and Rev. W. Chaplin
5	Henry Harris,	Convicted of Vagrancy the 2nd day of September, 1825. Ordered to be imprisoned and kept to hard labour Three Months.	F. J. B. Dashwood, Esq.
6	John Tidey,	Committed the 13th day of August, 1825, for not performing his Contract in making Bricks. Ordered to be imprisoned and kept to hard labour Three Months.	Rev. T. Roe and Rev. J. Mounsey
7	William Sight,	Committed the 15th day of August, 1825, for not obeying an order of Filiation. Ordered to be imprisoned and kept to hard labour Three Months.	John Bourne, Esq.
8	John Seamark,	Committed the 30th day of August, 1825, for not obeying an order of Filiation. Ordered to be imprisoned and kept to hard labour Three Months.	F. J. B. Dashwood, Esq.
9	Thomas Coney,	Committed the 1st day of September, 1825, for wilfully exposing his Person on the public Highway. Ordered to be imprisoned and kept to hard labour Three Months.	John Fytche, Esq.
10	James Walker,	Committed the 5th day of September, 1825, for wilfully damaging the Church-Yard Fence at Horncastle. Ordered to be imprisoned and kept to hard labour Two Calendar Months.	Rev. J. Mounsey
11	Thomas Cook,	Committed the 25th day of September, 1825, for refusing to obey the lawful commands of his Master. Ordered to be imprisoned and kept to hard labour One Calendar Month.	Rev. J. Mounsey and Rev. W. Goodenough
12	West Barnes,	Committed the 26th day of September, 1825, for leaving his Wife and Family chargeable to the parish of Bilsby. Ordered to be imprisoned and kept to hard labour Three Months.	F. J. B. Dashwood, Esq. and Rev. W. Dodson
13	Thomas Emerson,	Committed the 8th day of October, 1825, for leaving his Wife and Family chargeable to the parish of Alford. Ordered to be imprisoned and kept to hard labour Three Months.	Rev. W. Dodson
14	Solomon Waters,	Committed the 18th day of October, 1825, for refusing to finish his Work. Ordered to be imprisoned and kept to hard labour One Calendar Month.	Rev. E. Booth
15	Rebecca Westerby,	Committed the 13th day of September, 1825, for having had a Bastard Child chargeable to the parish of Saleby. Ordered to be imprisoned and kept to hard labour Three Calendar Months.	F. J. B. Dashwood, Esq. and Rev. W. Dodson
16	Susanna Arrowsmith,	Committed the 19th day of October, 1825, for refractory and improper behaviour in her Service. Ordered to be imprisoned and kept to hard labour One Month.	Rev. W. Dodson
17	William Whitworth,	Committed the 13th day of October, 1825, for want of Sureties in Bastardy.	Rev. J. Fretwell

Misdemeanants

Louth Calendar for the Michaelmas Sessions of 1825 records the names of 53 prisoners in the jail. Local magistrates had dealt with the 17 misdemeanants. Together with a dozen vagrants and debtors they continued to form a significant presence amongst the inmates of the prison.
LQS A/1/493/134 Lincolnshire Archives Office

a time, across the yard to their labour at the mill. Matron took the women to the laundry. Unconvicted prisoners were released in to the small airing yards where they had very little to do.

The dietary was monotonous, barely sufficient, and constantly tampered with by the justices. They tried to balance cost against intake and labour. Prisoners detained for less than four weeks were unlikely to suffer consequences of a meagre ration, but those on the wheel might loose weight rapidly. There was a pint of oatmeal gruel, a pound of bread, and milk from the keeper's cows for breakfast and supper every day, with gruel again for dinner with potatoes, and occasionally carrots and onions. Four ounces of meat was supplied on Sundays and Thursdays, and, inevitably, meat broth on Mondays and Fridays. With so much fluid in their diet, it's a wonder that the prison was not awash. The prisoners took their meals in the day rooms where they cooked potatoes on the stove. Victuals were brought from the keeper's kitchen and served out by the turnkey.

Twice a week the prison chaplain, Rev. Thomas A Dale held morning prayers when the prisoners and their officers assembled in the chapel above the keeper's lodging. The stalls were petitioned in a fan like shape about the pulpit with four pens for women and six for men. Occasionally there was a baptism. On Sundays there was a Divine Service with a full sermon, and books from the Society for Promotion of Christian Knowledge for the prisoners who could read. The chaplain interviewed new committals, and kept a journal of their religious knowledge and academic skill. Few could read and write well, and most had little spiritual understanding. Four times a year the Sacrament was taken, but only after the chaplain had examined the supplicants to his satisfaction. Other prisoners, including the sick, who wished to speak with the chaplain, could do so, but he did not normally visit the day rooms or punishment cells.

Prisoners returned from the mill at six o'clock for milk and 'cooked supper' served in the day rooms. An hour after sunset, the prison, and the prisoners, were locked up for the night.

The justices compounded several faults from the old house of correction. One of the most difficult omissions to understand was the absence of a bath for the inmates. At the very least some effort might have been taken to clean new admissions and, if necessary, 'stove' or fumigate their clothing. Poor physical health was often linked to an absence of hygiene, but with no reception area or facilities for medical examination by the surgeon, an opportunity to limit the spread of contagious disease was lost. This particularly applied to cases of 'the itch' amongst the vagrants who were detained in the old buildings in particularly close quarters. The most they might expect was a wash from a bucket of warm water.

From the surgeon's report to the prison inspectors; When a case of the itch occurs amongst the felons or misdemeanants they are immediately separated, but the vagrants are not; they are a mass of filth and dirt and all together. Some unfortunates amongst the 'mass of filth and dirt' were clean and of a distinctly better class.

Failure to provide an infirmary is also difficult to explain. Ulcerated legs, syphilis and gonorrhoea, and diarrhoea were prevalent amongst the inmates, the latter often leading to dysentery and death two to three weeks later. The surgeon advises the inspector: I am at a loss what to attribute it to (the diarrhoea); I ascribed it at one time to the lowness of the diet, but that was increased, and the cases still continue. There was a death this year from diarrhoea"

His journal recorded the condition of JS:
March 17th. JS. Very unwell; bilious fever.
March 19th. JS. Bilious vomiting and diarrhoea. In great danger.
March 25th. JS. No better. In imminent danger.
Same day, noon JS . The vomitings and diarrhoea had continued
with great violence, and he expired about noon.

They were mystified by the persistence of dysentery and similar illnesses, which were not present in the town. Often an inmate became poorly shortly after admission. They thought for some time an inadequate diet might be responsible, but an increase in provisions had little lasting effect. Once in the prison, typhus also spread rapidly, and in one outbreak, supposedly brought in by a vagrant, one of the turnkeys died.

Perhaps they needed to check the water supply. Cesspits for the privys surrounded the pump for prison drinking water. Both were a source of trouble. The well, and the pits, needed digging out regularly by local labourers. A stream was known to run beneath the prison. Little surprise therefore if sewage from so many inmates was contaminating the water supply.

The surgeon visited the prison about three times a week, more often if required by illness, and kept a journal of the treatment and health of his patients. In the absence of an infirmary, the sick were nursed in the day rooms, or wherever else may have been convenient. At Spilsby the infirmary was taken over by the magistrates as a kitchen, bathroom and surgery for their use at petty sessions.

At Louth visits to the prisoners took place at the wheel or in the airing yards. With little supervision, visitors were able to hand the inmates money, which they passed to the turnkeys who purchased items for them in the town. Those wishing to write letters were supplied with pen, ink and paper, mail being posted through the keeper.

That few could read or write well marked the need for instruction in simple skills, but the requirement was not attended to. The keeper claimed that some of the inmates who could read taught others willing to learn, but the choice of books, apart from a copy of Moore's

Almanac purchased for the prisoners by one of the officers, was limited. The prison needed a schoolmaster, and light employment for those not working on the wheel. The absence of rooms where the prisoners might receive useful instruction in reading and writing was a breach of Peel's Gaol Act, and placing day rooms at the end of the wings made supervision of the inmates well nigh impossible.

The prison faced other problems. With no increase in staff, or change in officers, when the new prison was opened, the gaol continued to be run in exactly the same way as the old house of correction. Without guidance from the justices, the officers simply carried old practises into the new gaol. Richard Cox and his wife Frances had run the House of Correction since they came to the Louth in 1808. They were both now in their 70s. The principle turnkey was a carpenter and joiner by trade, and at 50 years old unlikely to display the energy of a younger man. With few officers, the keeper needed the co-operation of the inmates for the gaol to function. Forced to compromise, the application of rigorous discipline was impossible. Given the circumstances of most of the inmates, the prison was unlikely to have any deterrent effect upon their behaviour. There was no attempt at reform. It is difficult to see what made the unruly so manageable. Cox's report for the Secretary of State for 1823 shows the two solitary or punishment cells had not been used nor had it been necessary to place a prisoner in irons or conduct a whipping. It remains to the credit of the keeper and his small staff that they were able to support and order the lives of those detained within the prison walls. Conditions may have been squalid, but the treatment of those in their care seems to have been humane.

The justices continued to approach their duties in the same way, and although committals for vagrancy varied greatly, those for minor breaches of the law increased. Despite the new gaol at Spilsby, conditions at Louth again became overcrowded, a further bar to improved discipline.

In 1829 the elderly Clerk of the Peace, Joseph Brackenbury, died, and the post of County Treasurer passed to Henry Pye, a successful local solicitor, town Assistant and Warden.

Central government was obliged to repeal much of the repressive control of public meetings and demonstrations that followed the riots at Peterloo. The death penalty for nearly 200 offences was abolished. Support for electoral reform and the repeal of the Corn Laws increased. If working people could not improve their lot by representation they might do so by revolution. The Swing riots of the 1830s, emanating from the discontent of the rural poor of southern England, spread to Lincolnshire. Hayricks and farms were set alight and new threshing machines destroyed. 365 special constables, including officers mounted on horseback, were sworn at the Spilsby

LINCOLNSHIRE,   LINDSEY, TO WIT.

Calendar of Prisoners
At Louth April Sessions,
HOLDEN the 20th DAY of APRIL 1833.

PRISONERS.	AGE.	When Committed. 1833.	OFFENCES.	Committing Magistrates.	SENTENCES.
1 Isaac Simpson,	22	Feb. 4th,	Stealing at Louth, Twelve Cards of Edging, and other Articles, the property of James Holbrook.	Henry Pye, Esq.	Nine Calendar Months H. L.
2 Joseph Neeve,	24	Feb. 28th,	Stealing at Louth, One Cloak, the property of Francis Frankish, and One Cloak, the property of Harriet Moody.	Henry Pye, Esq.	Nine Calendar Months H. L.
3 James Lindsey,	50	March 5th,	Stealing at Louth, One Silver Table Spoon, the property of Ann Hewins.	J. T. Banks, Esq.	Twelve Calendar Months H. L.
4 William Thompson,	24	April 19th,	Stealing at Louth, a Purse, half a Sovereign, Nine Shillings in Silver, and other Articles, from the Person of Henry Borrell.	J. T. Banks, Esq.	Transported Seven Years.
5 Richard Jordan, 6 Robert Holt,		April 20th,	Stealing at Louth, one Pair of White Cotton Stockings, the property of James Harrison.	J. Fytche, Esq.	Transported Seven Years.

CONVICTED PRISONERS.

		1833.			
1 Mary Ann Hatcliff, 2 Mary Ann Belton,		Jan. 29th,	Sureties to be of good behaviour. Six Calendar Months each.		H. Pye, Esq. and J. T. Banks, Esq.
3 William Simmons, 4 Ann Simmons, his Wife,		Jan. 29th.	Keeping a Disorderly House. Twelve Calendar Months each.		H. Pye, Esq. and J. T. Banks, Esq.
5 Bridget Milson,		Feb. 8th,	Bastardy. Twelve Calendar Months.	-	H. Pye, Esq. and E. L'Oste, Esq.
6 Elizabeth Parker,		March 1st,	Bastardy. Twelve Calendar Months.	-	H. Pye, Esq. and W. Allison, Esq.
7 Timothy Harness Lawrence,		Jan. 15th,	Felony. Six Calendar Months, H. L.		
8 Tyson Hardiman,		Jan. 15th,	Felony. Twelve Calendar Months, H. L. The first and last fortnights solitary.		By the Court; F. Lucas, Clerk of the Peace.
9 John Kirk, the Younger,		April 19th,	Misdemeanor. One Calendar Month, H. L.		Henry Pye, Esq.
10 Thomas Hall,		April 19th,	Bastardy. Want of Sureties.	-	J. T. Banks, Esq.
11 William Allbones,		April 19th,	Assault.	-	J. T. Banks, Esq.

VAGRANTS.

1 William Clayton,	March 21st,	One Calendar Month H. L.	-	J. T. Banks, Esq.
2 Charles Leaser,	March 21st,	One Calendar Month H. L.	-	W. Allison, Esq.
3 James Wood,	March 22nd,	One Calendar Month H. L.	-	J. T. Banks, Esq.
4 John Brown,	March 22nd,	One Calendar Month H. L.	-	J. T. Banks, Esq.
5 William Farrier,	March 23rd,	One Calendar Month H. L.	-	J. T. Banks, Esq.
6 Ann Smith, 7 John, her Son,	March 30th,	One Calendar Month	-	H. Pye, Esq.
8 George Smith,	April 3rd,	One Calendar Month	-	H. Pye, Esq.
9 William Armstrong,	April 3rd,	One Calendar Month H. L.	-	J. T. Banks, Esq.
10 John Marshall,	April 6th,	Twenty-one Days.	-	J. T. Banks, Esq.
11 John Farrier,	April 11th,	One Calendar Month H. L.	-	W. Allison, Esq.
12 William James,	April 12th,	One Calendar Month H. L.	-	J. T. Banks, Esq.
13 Andrew Miller,	April 16th,	One Calendar Month H. L.	-	J. T. Banks, Esq.
14 Susan Allbones,	April 19th,	One Calendar Month H. L.	-	J. T. Banks, Esq.
15 Mary Carey,	April 19th,	One Calendar Month H. L.	-	J. T. Banks, Esq.
16 John Hall,	April 19th,	One Calendar Month H. L.	-	Edward L'Oste, Esq.
17 Mary Collins,	April 19th,	Three Calendar Months H. L.	-	J. T. Banks, Esq.
18 Richard Toyne,	April 19th,	Three Calendar Months H. L.	-	J. T. Banks, Esq.

[Jacksons, Printers, Louth.]   **RICHARD COX, Gaoler.**

Prison Calendar, 1833
PCOM 2/439
Public Record Office, Kew

Sessions and issued with lettered and numbered staffs.

The Reform Bill of 1832 was less than satisfactory. With the vote extended to male tenants of property with a rental value of more than £10 a year, only the middle classes were to benefit. The working poor were bitterly disappointed, but the Act established a precedent for extending the franchise to other classes at a later date. Local government reform followed three years later.

There had long been concern at the variable nature of local government in Britain, particularly in the chartered boroughs such as Louth, where non-elected officials – the wardens - wielded considerable power. Alongside industrious and up-standing officials were those only too keen to make decisions in their own best interests rather than those of the townspeople. In a report on Louth, the Parliamentary commissioners commended the work of the Warden and his Assistants in establishing a woollen manufactury in the town. Though never profitable, the production of worsted, blankets, carpets and rugs provided a local market for the long coarse wool from large flocks of Lincolnshire Longwool sheep on the Wolds, and work for more than a hundred families. They deemed *'the appearance of the town is very respectable'*, but noted that no tradesman had ever been invited to become a member of the Corporation.

The Municipal Corporations Act of 1835 established a more democratic system in the 178 chartered boroughs of England and Wales. In Louth, the ratepayers now elected 18 Councillors who in turn chose the Mayor. Not surprisingly there was some friction between members of the old corporation, (who retained stewardship of the Grammar School), and the new Council. The former Assistants were wealthy and powerful men in their own right, and continued to serve as town justices.

Inspection by His Majesty's Inspector of Prisons in 1837 revealed the gaol to have a number of shortcomings. He found the prison neither clean nor tidy. Bundles of clothes and provisions lay about the day rooms, where marks on the tables suggested gambling by the inmates. There was scribbling on the cell walls, and figures and letters carved on the boards of the treadwheel. The prison was crowded and noisy. There were no rules enforcing silence. Rules for the operation of the prison had not been changed since first published in 1809. It made little difference. Regulations had little bearing on the way in which the House of Correction functioned. The House was run as well as the constraints of the building permitted. 'Rules' were for the benefit of central government and her inspectors, not for the guidance and protection of the inmates and their officers.

The women's cells were so close to the men's that they were able to call to them from their part of the prison. Conversation was of a loose order. Prostitutes from Louth were especially refractory. There was

Gas-light and coke
Just one gas lamp. Candles for the rest of the prison.
**Lindsey Quarter Sessions A/1/578/39
Lincolnshire Archives Office**

talking on the wheel, and in the cells at night. The mill, with a lath and plaster roof, was insecure, and labour little more than minimal. Failure to complete the new treadwheels in the main body of the prison was regrettable. Inmates not subject to 'hard labour' lay about the airing yards or played games. He recommended the supply of food and other provisions be put out to contract, and that cooking in the day rooms should cease.

The Prison Inspector was told by the surgeon: *The working classes in this immediate neighbourhood live well, perhaps better than in most parts of England. Upon the low scale of diet (in the prison) the men lost flesh and were unable to do their work at the wheel. Extreme debility ensued. I had the prisoners weighed and they lost weight so rapidly that I was compelled to make a representation to the magistrates, and the diet now in use was substitute.*

Food was sometimes used as barter. Debtors were unfairly subject to the same 'restraint' as the prisoners. The solitary cells for punishment in the old house of correction were below ground, damp and without lighting, did not bare inspection and remained unfit for their purpose. (At Kirton, where the interior of the punishment cells was painted black, they were referred to as the 'dark' cells).

The Inspector found little zeal or vigour displayed by the officers. He particularly notes that Frances Cox, the matron, was 74 years old. Helped in some of her duties by a female relative, she rarely attended divine service. Deaf and almost blind, she was no longer suited to her office. His report suggested there was considerable room for improvement in the House of Correction at Louth.

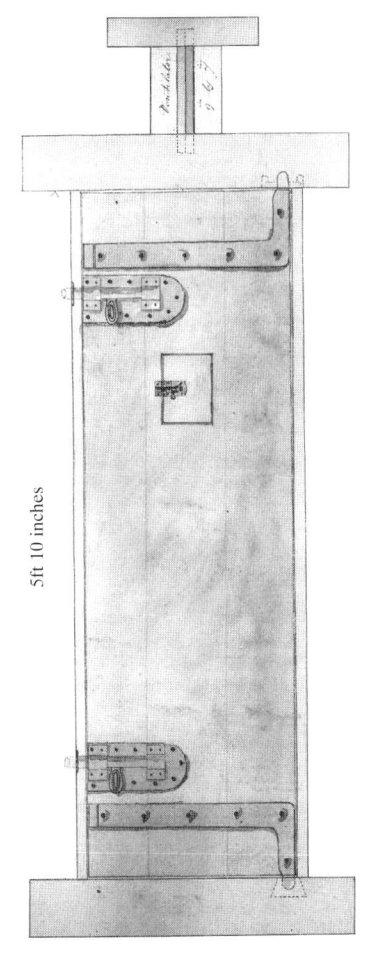

Cell Door

To the Worshipful Her Majesty's Justices of the Peace acting for the Louth and Spilsby Subdivision of the Parts of Lindsey

Gentlemen

The growing age and infirmities of My Wife and myself admonish us to retire from the Office of Matron and Keeper of the House of Correction at Louth which we have been permitted to hold under you for upwards of 30 years altho' during that long service I have been enabled to make some provision for my old age yet as I am not in circumstances to live without assistance I beg respectfully to solicit that you will be kind enough to exercise in my favour the provisions of the Gaol act which authorises you to bestow an annuity on an aged and superannuated Gaoler to such extent as you may think ~~requires~~ the length and character of my services may deserve –

I propose if agreeable to you to give up the situation at the next April Sessions and am

Gentlemen
with great respect
Your most Obedient
humble Servant

Rich.d Cox

April 23.rd 1838

Richard Cox's resignation
A most dignified letter given the circumstances of his departure
**Lindsey Quarter Sessions A/1/590/35
Lincolnshire Archives Office**

-9-

Beyond Redemption

PRISON inspectors were appointed by His Majesty's Commissioners in London. They were to visit the various prisons of Great Britain and report on the conditions they found to both houses of parliament. They were part of the move towards social reform. Their reports to central government influenced local practise and went some way towards improving the living conditions of prisoners detained in the nations gaols.

The judiciary in Lincolnshire, ultimately responsible for conditions in the county's prisons, had no wish to be found wanting in the way in which they carried out their responsibilities. They took the inspector's recommendations seriously, and appointed committees to advise the justices of the best way to implement suggestions. Not all proposals were adopted.

The journals, comments and opinions of those working in the nation's gaols formed an important part of the information collected by the prison inspectors during their visits. Prison staff soon realised that requests and suggestions made direct to their own governing bodies, often ignored or discounted, carried more weight if the ideas were taken up by the inspector and included in his report.

When Captain William John Williams returned to Louth in November 1839 he was encouraged to find the superannuated keeper and matron in office at the time of his last visit had been replaced. He trusted the new governor, John Brian, would improve the prison's discipline when remaining deficiencies had been addressed. There was little else to please him.

In his report, Williams found the cells to be generally clean, but the bedding not. There were bundles of clothing, food and rubbish lying about. He found the condition of the vagrants deplorable. All were dirty and several without shirts or shoes. Some infected with the itch were working on the wheel. He recorded the chaplain saying, *The dirt and filth of the vagrants is almost intolerable.*

One of the turnkeys explained, *The felons and vagrants are together on the mill. Clean shirts are not issued. I have observed them most filthy when going to Chapel. I have known men to catch the itch; one vagrant gives it to another.*

His colleague supported him: *I have heard prisoners complain of the vagrants walking with them, and being in the same room with them when they have the itch. There are very few that have more than one shirt on their back, and they have to go without till it is washed.*

He was told by the matron: *Great inconvenience is felt amongst the females for the want of gaol clothing; they are obliged to lie in bed until their linen is washed.*

The Inspector found the punishment cells to be wretched places. Located beneath the old buildings and out of hearing of the rest of the prison, it was difficult to know how a man or woman taken ill in the solitary cells at night could make themselves heard. Since the inspector's last visit, breaches of discipline – fighting, shouting, misbehaving in chapel - have resulted in 40 instances of solitary confinement, and nine whippings. Most confinement is for six hours, but 24 hours is not unusual. 20 – 25 lashes is the norm for a whipping, more normally ordered by the court.

One of the turnkeys was using the treadmill to crush beans. The transaction was not recorded in the accounts, and the work was clearly being carried out for private profit.

A number of the inmates are sick. They suffered from hernias, dropsy, asthma, consumption and, inevitably, diarrhoea. The sick were nursed, and sometimes died, in the day rooms. John Johnson, a 24-year old felon, had been in the prison for more than two years with ulcerated legs and diseased bones.

During the past year there had been four deaths in the House. One, an infant born in prison, suffered convulsions. A 65-year old had a diseased heart, and two youngsters died of consumption and syphilis. Caroline Staples was committed to the prison suffering from consumption and syphilis. She was found collapsed in the street. The chaplain records the death *of this poor creature ... living an abandoned life* ten days after her admission. She was 18 years old. All three adults were in a state of utter exhaustion when brought to the prison, a not unusual occurrence. This helps explain the high number of deaths in the House. Inmates did not die because they were in prison; they remained in prison beyond the term of their sentence because they were expected to breathe their last.

Standards are no better at Kirton.

Captain Williams found a number of other issues wanting, and brought them to the notice of the magistrates before his departure. His inspection marked a low point in the prisons operation, and may have brought home to some of the justices the extent of their responsibilities, and the degree to which they were failing. Within four weeks the justices instructed the keeper to write to the Commissioners. He was to advise them that the visiting magistrates, in compliance with the Inspector's suggestions, had directed a bath be installed and reception rooms provided. Fumigation apparatus was to be purchased and an itch ward prepared. Sufficient clothing, possibly a uniform dress, was to be found for all the prisoners. The chaplain was to read prayers daily, and the surgeon was to examine all prisoners on admission and make regular checks on other inmates.

It was intended the prison should slowly evolve into a place of disciplined punishment and detention for those the community found difficult to control. One of the gaol's key roles, that of safety net for the feckless poor, was slowly transferred to the Workhouse and its infirmary on Holmes Lane. Those 'on the tramp' retained some independence by admission to the Workhouse, whilst the needs of young children were more readily suited by the presence, on paper at least, of a schoolmaster and mistress. In consequence, the profile of the prison's inmates changed.

The census for 1841 records 49 people in the prison at the beginning of June; 36 were prisoners, the rest officers and their families. Living with the master, matron and their 13-year old daughter, Jane, in the keepers dwelling were three other people: Eliza Holgarth, their servant, William Chatterton, the miller, and Elizabeth Burbidge, the newly appointed female turnkey. The cost of the turnkey's board was deducted from her salary, which was halved to £4 11s (£4.55p) a quarter. In the gatehouse with John Maxey, the chief turnkey, and his wife Harriet, were their son a carpenter, and grandson. The under turnkey, Edward Abbott, probably lodged in the gate-house by the mill with his wife Ann, but was often required to sleep overnight in the new prison. The prison staff numbered six.

The female prisoners were all young, three were teenagers. Mary Horwell, the oldest at 21, and Charlotte Whitworth, aged 15, were common prostitutes. Horwell had been confined in the House of Correction for nearly 18 months. She had served her sentence, but would not be released until she found sureties for her good behaviour. This was a common occurrence. Ann Holstein awaited trial for theft, but would be discharged. Hannah Cuthbert, just 13 years old and the youngest in the prison, had been convicted of stealing two china mugs in Louth and was just beginning a three-month sentence.

Female prisoners, other than those committed as vagrants, occupied the cells in the east wing, the opposite side of the keeper's house to the old house of correction. Convicted women were on the ground floor. They were set to mending clothes, needlework and preparing meals, or work in the washhouse and laundry at the gate, where they were unsupervised. Women awaiting trial were housed on the first floor of

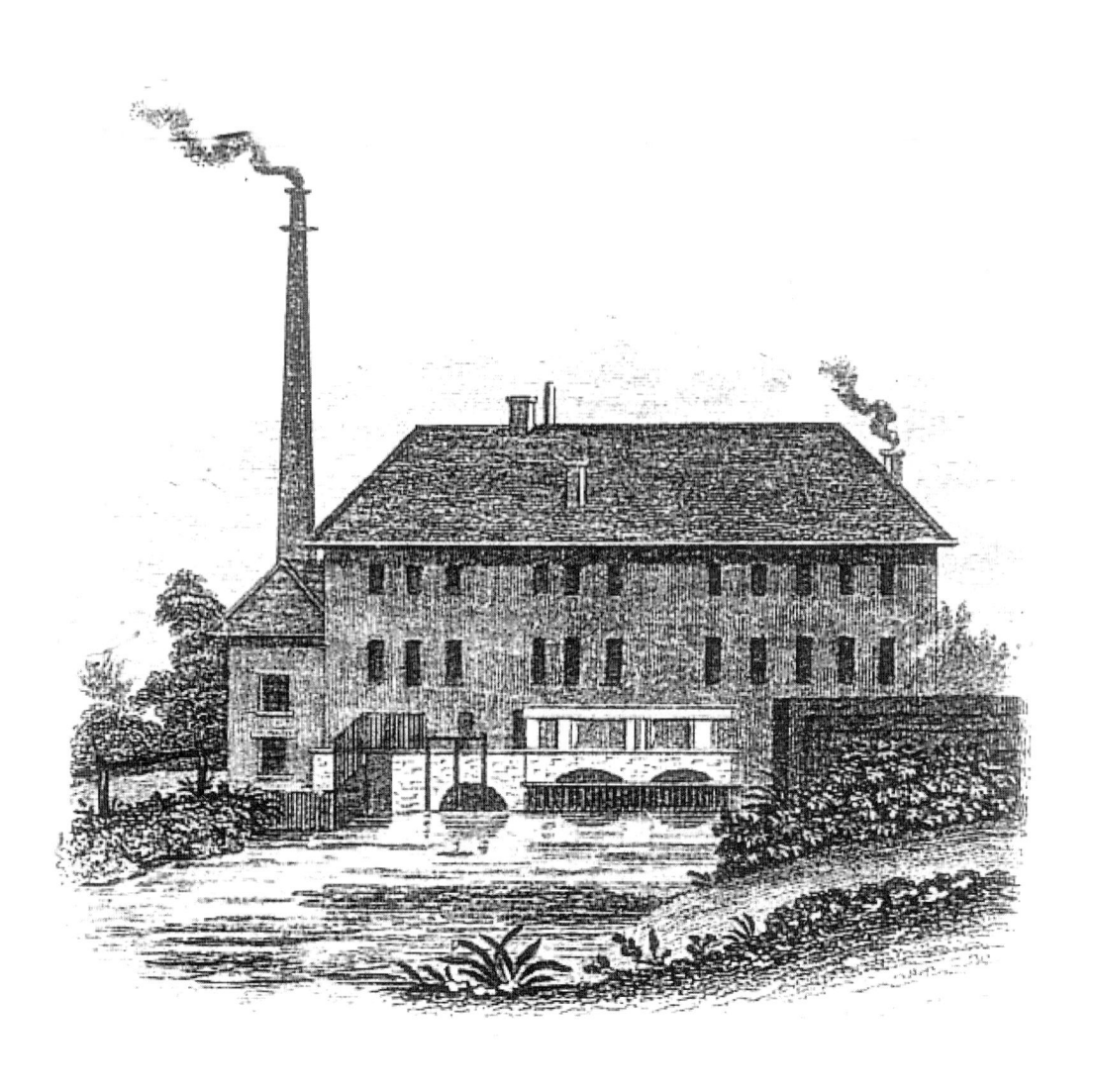

Carpet and Blanket Manufactory 1841
Built by Louth Corporation to provide work for the poor, but later sold into private hands. The steam engine was a recent addition.
**Lindsey Quarter Sessions A/1/614/27
Lincolnshire Archives Office**

the wing along with the debtors. They were not required to work, but usually wished to do so. The top floor was used as an infirmary, and for the detention of juvenile female offenders to *separate and keep them apart from older and more depraved characters*. The women were provided with a slipper bath in the laundry, and a new washhouse was built in the female airing yard. The chaplain provided books in their day room.

The surgeon examined all new committals *if their condition warranted it*, and *if necessary through vermin, filth or disease* they were washed or cleaned in a warm - or cold - bath. The washroom in the lodge had been converted into a bathhouse and reception for male prisoners. Issued with prison clothing, their own was taken from them to be fumigated, stored and returned on discharge. Before they joined the other prisoners the men's hair was cut. Combs, scissors and razors were added to the prison inventory.

Male prisoners were housed in the north wing. At the time of the census in 1841, more than half the men were under the age of 25, and most were petty thieves. Tobacco, a red silk handkerchief, a nightcap and stockings, a silver watch, and five strikes of wheat were amongst the items they stole. Job Lound, a groom, had taken a saddle and bridle. For several of the thieves a whipping, administered in the prison by the keeper, formed part of the sentence. Whilst some inmates were labourers, a chimney sweep, shoemaker, butcher, clerk and mariner were among other occupations recorded. Two had embezzled small sums of cash from their employers. Several of the older men were skilled and had been local traders. They included a wheelwright, cotton spinners, and silk and carpet weavers. West Barnes, a 50-year old carpenter, had not paid his taxes and was in prison for debt. Imprisonment for debt for sums of less than £20 would shortly be abolished. Thomas Stiles, a blacksmith, was serving two years imprisonment for assaulting six-year old Ann Johnson *with intent to unlawfully and carnally know and abuse her*. As an assault the case was treated as a misdemeanour. The oldest inmate was 70-years old George Dawson.

Although none of the inmates were recorded in the census as vagrants, 20-year old James Thompson had been in the House of Correction since the beginning of October as *a rogue and vagabond*. His committal under that section of the Vagrancy Act indicates it was not his first conviction. His sentence of three calendar months imprisonment with hard labour may have been an act of compassion by the justices rather than any attempt at reform or punishment. He was a very sick man. Rather than discharge him at the end of his sentence in January with a shilling, as was the practise with sick prisoners, he remained in the gaol. At the surgeons direction he receives additional diet, milk, ale or porter, tobacco and wine. He was cared for in the prison until his death in the middle of June.

John Johnson's case was unusual. Convicted of stealing a boat from a builder at Great Grimsby, he was serving a sentence of seven years transportation. John Johnson pleaded 'not guilty' when he appeared before the court in October 1838, but the evidence against him was compelling. Johnson, two other men and a woman, were seen to take a small sailing boat from Boiling House Creek, Great Grimsby at high tide by two men sitting on the bank. They knew the boat to belong to a local ship builder, William Shaw. With the wind blowing tolerably strong from the southeast, they watched as the boat moved out into the Humber under sail, against the ebb, towards Hull. Having told the owner what they had seen and learned that the vessel had been taken without his consent, one of the witnesses, William Self, travelled to Hull the following Tuesday. He found the boat moored to the stern of a sloop owned by a local coal trader and called the constable.

John Grayburns, a coal dealer, said he was present when Johnson offered the boat to a colleague for two pounds. Johnson told them he was poorly and going into the infirmary, which may have been true. He said he needed to be shot of the boat. After some words, and examination of the boat and its fittings, Grayburn's offer of 35 shillings (£1.75p) was accepted. The value of the property taken including stores, rigging, mast, sail, oars, anchor and cable totalled more the £12, a considerable sum for the sessions. 20 years earlier a thief might well have been dealt with at the county assize and hung for his folly.

Johnson gave no explanation for his conduct to the committing magistrate. Perhaps he had not taken the boat but did not have an alibi. What of the three others present in the vessel when she was taken? Did Johnson take their punishment? We shall never know.

The criminal population were thought to fear *the leaving of the country*, but by the 1840s it was becoming increasingly difficult to secure a passage for 'transports' to Australia. The abolition of capital punishment for many serious offences now meant they took priority over lesser convictions. Prisoners sentenced to less than 15 years transportation increasingly served their sentences in the prison hulks or local gaols. This was especially so if they were deemed unlikely to survive the journey, or to be of little use on arrival. Johnson may have been saved by his poor physical condition. Removal of convicts to the hulks by public conveyance proved *a source of great evil*. If the time of departure was known, a crowd of associates and onlookers often besieged the gates of the gaol. Of three men and one woman sentenced to transportation by the Lindsey justices that sessions, only one man is eventually landed in New South Wales to serve 15 years 'beyond the seas'.

As transports were not sentenced to hard labour, they could not be forced to work on the wheel. The governor, or keeper of the prison, appointed Johnson, who at the time of his conviction was 22 years old, as one of those to nurse and wait upon the sick. He could read and write, and the keeper allowed him pen, ink and paper. No doubt he wrote and read letters for others in the prison. With his ulcerated legs and diseased bones he was allowed an enhanced diet, alcohol and tobacco as with other sick prisoners, under the directions of the prison surgeon.

Thomas A Dale, the prison chaplain, had mixed feelings about him. Whilst he commended those selected to nurse the sick, he noted that Johnson's temper has not been softened by his confinement. He believed it unlikely that such protracted imprisonment would result in the man's reform.

The new prison was planned to separate the prisoners. The justices soon realised both day rooms and cells could be used as sleeping wards. The day rooms took four double beds and slept eight prisoners. 'Single' cells, packed with a single and double bed, might sleep three. A day room was provided for the turnkeys, one of whom slept in the main prison at night.

In the old house of correction, where the vagrants were left day and night without an officer, a small room was fitted up as an itch ward with fumigation equipment for clothes, and the old chapel was used as their infirmary. Four larger rooms were filled with beds according to the number of inmates. For the justices of Louth, the prevalence of vagrancy within the county often threatened to overwhelm them. In some desperation they agreed to award constables three shillings and six pence (17p) for each vagrant committed to the prison. It was hoped the remuneration would encourage them in the discharge of their duties. For the Clerk of the Court, there is two shillings (10p) a case. Not surprisingly, the numbers did not fall. A cell is set aside for the admission of prisoners arriving at the gaol late at night.

Young children and their mothers were now more likely to be found in the Union Workhouse. This was not always to their taste. From the journal kept by the chaplain, Thomas A Dale: 17 Nov 1841 *J.Dawson, a woman committed as a vagrant, with four children, one at the breast, one with measles, quite enceinte (pregnant); says her husband, a baker, left her a year ago; came from Leeds about a month since, and has been in the Louth union; did not like it because her children were taken from her, and one, she thought, not used well; she prefers a prison; else could go back to the union; did not suffer much with distress coming from Leeds; one child, William, died subsequently, December 3rd 1841.*

The role of prison chaplain was an unenviable one. As a salaried member of the staff, he alone was responsible for the moral improvement of the inmates. It seems likely the justices wished nothing more to do with those they had so quickly imprisoned, yet gave the chaplain Thomas Dale little support with his task.

In his reports to the magistrates, he constantly brought to their attention the absence of activities available to those not subject to hard labour. Inaction in the dayrooms brought about disputes and minor disturbances. This was especially so amongst those awaiting trial, or excused the wheel by the surgeon on account of their physical condition.

By his own enquiries he knew that few of the prisoners could read or write well. He realised it was unlikely those on short sentences could be taught to read, but thought that several might benefit from the provision of elementary books of instruction in recovering reading skills they had lost. The few old books that were available were well used, but in poor condition. If more might be purchased, including bibles and prayer books, the moral and religious knowledge of the prisoners might be improved.

As the prison chaplain, Dale fervently believed *the only effectual method of counteracting the attempts of wicked and designing men to undermine the principles of the lower classes and render them discontented …is the diffusion of sound Religious Knowledge, in which there can be no excess … that all may be taught that obedience to the laws of the land and the government of the country is due, not as a matter of compulsion, but on principle and conscience.*

He examined all prisoners on their way of life. He found most had little knowledge or concern for religion. About a third claimed to be dissenters from the Anglican Church. Forced by poverty to commence manual labour at an early age to support themselves, their mental and moral education was not complete and they became candidates for the house of correction. With too much idle time in the prison, they needed a schoolmaster. This was certainly no wish to educate 'the lower classes' in order they might improve their prospects in life. There was a strongly held belief that prisoners were sent to the House of Correction for punishment, not education. Others realised that if no attempt was made to provide the inmates with skills to sustain a future livelihood they were labouring in vain. When their liberty was restored they had *no alternative but to return to their former vicious habits*.

Dale thought it was difficult to see what lasting benefits accrued from their time in prison, and believed the 'silent system', worked elsewhere, of doubtful value. He did not usually visit those in solitary confinement. He found the prisoners well behaved in chapel, though this may have been attributed to the presence of the governor, matron and officers. Sometimes he found them troublesome. The vagrants knew where he lived and eventually he was obliged to tell them it was quite beyond his power to do anything for them.

He told the prisons Inspector: *Notwithstanding the mixed character of the major part of the Congregation in the Chapel of Louth House of Correction, their too generally irreligious habits, their equally general ignorance, with few exceptions, of anything beyond the name of*

Christianity ... the Demeanour of Prisoners on all occasions of Public Religious Worship is marked by silent and uniform attention. Awe, deference, insolence or resignation to their condition? One feels that the chaplain's was a hopeless task.

Visits by the Inspector brought other changes. Contracts for provisions, bread, flour, oatmeal, oxheads, bones and beef, potatoes and coal were advertised and orders placed with tradespeople in the town. J. Mawer, butcher, provided cheeks and shanks, and every week John Griffin delivered 50 stones of bread to the new gaol. Provisions were weighed and inspected by the keeper who might return unsatisfactory goods.

Changes to the diet were only to be made on the advice of the surgeon. There should be no more than two ounces of oatmeal in every pint of gruel. Too great a consistency disordered the digestive organs. When the diet was criticised for containing too much fluid, beef was substituted for boiled oxheads and bones in the summer, and the soups and broths were seasoned or thickened with salt, vegetables and peppers. Vagrants, and those sentenced to less than two months detention, receive less food than other inmates. The sick - one prisoner in five needed medical attention - were given an enhanced diet including butter, eggs, milk, tea, vinegar, ginger, potatoes and tobacco. One of the prisoners was appointed cook.

Plans to remove the treadwheels to the sheds provided in the new prison were deferred. The printing of a set of rules was thought unnecessary as the justices operated the prison, as far as they are able, within the requirements of the law. The pressing need to occupy the time of those not set to hard labour was ignored.

Other matters continued to trouble the justices. The sewers at both prisons were completely choked up and obstructed. An offensive and unwholesome effluvia pervaded the eastern end of town. The drains were cleaned out and traps fitted to prevent the circulation of foul air. (Dry rot was found at Spilsby, where the salary of the miller, who had left, continued to be claimed).

When the surgeon, Francis Overton, was told of his additional duties, he resigned. John Bogg, already attending paupers in the workhouse, was appointed in his place.

In 1842 the petty sessions were transferred from the town to a magistrates courthouse newly built within the prison enclosure. The justices soon realised they could use the new building for the first day of sessions, now given over to civil and financial business. Reports of the visiting committees were considered, jury lists checked, costs claimed for the prosecution of offenders and transportation of convicts examined, contracts and tenders for supplies and work in the house confirmed, and salaries and accounts settled. The records of the treasurer were audited and allowed, and a rate set for the following quarters.

John Hurst, Chemist, Mercer Row, Louth
*Dispensed prescriptions, horse medicines, perfumery, cigars, candles and pickles.
John Hurst provided the prison with soap, linseed oil and red lead paint.*
**Lindsey Quarter Sessions A/1/650/8
Lincolnshire Archives Office**

NOTICE TO LADIES.

—oo—

Mrs. Brogden has now nearly 80 Servants Registered for May Day, including Housekeepers, good Plain Cooks, Housemaids, Sewing Maids, General Servants, Nursemaids, etc.

An early application is solicited.

Louth Gazette, October 1869

The magistrates were directed that vagrants, now more regularly dealt with at petty sessions, were not to be detained for more than 14 days in the House of Correction, and could expect a meagre diet. The constable's bounty was reduced to a shilling.

From the Sessions minutes, January 1842: *Ordered that in future the following diet be allowed to persons committed to the House of Correction at Louth and Spilsby for offences under the Vagrancy Act*:

	Breakfast and Supper	*Dinner*
Sunday	One quart of oatmeal porridge and half a pound of bread	One quart of stew of Heads and bones with half a pound of potatoes
Monday	The same	One quart of oatmeal porridge
Tuesday	The same	Same as Sunday
Wednesday	The same	Same as Monday
Thursday	The same	Five ounces of beef without bone after boiling and one pound of potatoes
Friday	The same	One quart of broth from the beef of Thursday with leeks or onions and a quarter of an ounce of oatmeal for each prisoner
Saturday	The same	The same as on Monday

As with the occasional publication of prison rules, in practise such tables were merely a starting point. As the main constituent was water, the amount of solids was infinitely variable. Stews and broths are thickened with potatoes, carrots and onions. In general, if prisoners lost weight, or became ill, their diet was increased.

The prison inspector was concerned that the new court prevented completion of the prison to the original plan - the third wing. Without more accommodation the inmates must continue to sleep together in the same beds. He questioned the wisdom of placing the court quite so close to the jail.

In October, the body of William Gibbons was found when the sleeping wards of the vagrant prison were unlocked in the morning. He was an epileptic subject to daily attacks, and normally sat for the greater part of the day with a turnkey in the watch room for the mill. The following month, 24-year old Patrick McKennan, another vagrant, ill since admission with consumption, also died.

In December two men awaiting trial, Thomas Smith and George Melton, escaped from the prison by climbing over their airing yard wall and walking out of a back door left open for workmen in the new building. A third man stopped by the watchman was placed in solitary confinement for three days on a bread and water diet. The subsequent enquiry found no one to blame. With three gates to guard, and few staff, the escape was deemed an accident. A watchman, or gatekeeper, often a turnkey's wife, was to be employed night and day.

By contrast the justices were obliged to write to George Hildeyard Tennyson D'Eyncourt, one of their magistrates at Tealby, after two men committed by him for vagrancy, presented themselves at the door of the house of Correction, bearing their warrant, but unattended by a constable, having made their own way to Louth. No matter how desperate conditions in the jail, for some it remained better than life outside.

Louth was now a thriving market town. Not only the centre of a union of 88 parishes under the new Poor Law, but a polling place for parliamentary elections in Lindsey. In 40 years the number of inhabitants had doubled to more than 9,000 people. A Wool Mart complimented the carpet and blanket manufactuary. The River Lud drove a paper mill at the west end of town. Gas from the coking plant at Riverhead lit more than 150 street lamps. Granaries and wharves on the canal serviced a growing trade in local produce.

The town's success also brought problems, particularly at the time of the spring and autumn fairs. Hustling and rowdyism became the order of the day. Stalls were pilfered and pockets picked. Unruly youths, supposedly the children of casuals and trampers, beset the markets, dividing the spoils later in their lodging house rooms. Beer houses and prostitution flourished. Lewd and disorderly women ran lewd and disorderly houses. Cockfighting, dog baiting, jugglers and cardsharps drew riotous crowds. There were fears for the morals of the town's youth.

The failure of the potato crop in Ireland in 1845, and two consecutive years of failed harvests at home enabled Robert Peel to abolish the Corn Laws. Fears that agriculture would slide into depression proved unfounded. Imports of grain from Europe were more than outweighed by greater demand for food supplies from a growing population and the newly industrialised towns. Farming became more efficient with greater use of steam power to drive heavy equipment, and the introduction of artificial fertilisers. The benefits of free trade were acknowledged.

Turnpikes, bridges and canals that had so opened up the county at the end of the previous century were about to be joined by a competitor, the railways. As the movement of goods and passengers became cheaper and speedier, the expence of maintaining a dozen small prisons for the three parts of the county came ever more into question.

The enthusiasm of the magistrates for imprisoning many of those brought before them showed no sign of abating. By 1848 the daily average of those detained in Louth House of Correction, mostly men, was 79, the greatest number on any one day being 149. If the laws against vagrancy continued to be enforced with such vigour, expansion of the prison was required immediately.

The visiting prison inspector, Mr D. O'Brien, wrote personally to the justices that year expressing concern at the overcrowding, the absence of instruction for those not on the wheel, and the inadequate nature of the prison design. He was especially concerned at illegal practise of sleeping two inmates in a bed. John Brian, the keeper was not well. He had erysipelas, - St Anthony's Fire – a reddening of the facial skin. Dr Bogg, the surgeon, wrote to the justices advising a change of air to be beneficial and a temporary replacement was engaged.

J.S. Padley, the county surveyor, produced plans for the jail adding a fourth storey, a third wing, and an elaborate circular dwelling, a panopticon, for the vagrants. Improving accommodation for the prisoners was not seen by a majority of the justices as a matter of importance, and no action was taken.

In 1849 they extend the magistrate's court, at a cost of £1,500, to enable the Quarter Sessions to sit in the same building. When Holy Trinity Church is rebuilt in 1866, divine service was conducted there. By doubling the size of the courthouse, land that might have been available for the prison's extension was lost.

Overcrowding reduced the effectiveness of the gaol as a place of punishment or reform. No matter how good the staff, and there were few enough of them, the maintenance of discipline was extremely difficult. The limitations of the building, in particular the shortage of living space, meant there was little hope of separating the different classes of prisoner. Young and old, those already sentenced and suspects awaiting trial, vagrant, debtor, misdemeanant and felon were all mixed hopelessly together.

The treasurer Henry Pye warned the justices the county fund was at risk of not being able to meet all payments due. The expense incurred in operating the prisons of Lindsey exceeded the rate collected. The justices authorised him to borrow, from time to time, such money as may be necessary to fulfil their obligations. A suggestion by Frederick Hill, the prison Inspector, that an independent auditor be appointed to appraise the prisons account was considered neither expedient nor necessary.

For those sentenced to hard labour, and most prison sentences carried this tag, there were insufficient places on the wheel. This was probably a blessing as the dietary was now so carefully controlled that

106

Petty and Sessions Court
*The magistrate's court was built in 1842.
Part of the old House of Correction was demolished seven years later
to make room for a quarter sessions court next door.*
**Lindsey Quarter Sessions B/5/Louth Box 2 1849
Lincolnshire Archives Office**

it was expected the health of men set to the wheel for 12 months hard labour would be giving way by the end of their sentence.

For those not sentenced to hard labour, recognition was given of the need to provide alternative activities. Two sheds behind the airing yards, originally intended for the treadwheels, were extended to form a covered space 95 feet long. Tailors, carpenters and shoemakers amongst the inmates were set to work here at their profession. There was mat and brush making, oakum and horsehair picking, and bookbinding and repairing. Supervision was much better, and 'silence' imposed upon those at labour. Part of the room was set aside as a dining hall for the convicted men and for use as a schoolroom for those under instruction. Prisoners continued to cook the food and nurse the sick, and clean and whitewash the building. One of the prison inspectors, O'Brien, notes, the old house of correction, though dilapidated in appearance and full to overflowing, was kept scrupulously clean. There were no complaints!

One of the turnkeys was appointed schoolmaster with two hours school instruction in the morning and two hours after dinner. All the prisoners except the vagrants attended at least once a week. About half the committals to prison were illiterate. The schoolmaster gave instruction in reading and spelling, writing and arithmetic. The chaplain provided books from the Society for the Promotion of Christian Knowledge. It was hoped that proficient inmates might help others. Instruction was also given in geography, history and the catechisms of the Church of England.

Overcrowding, and a shortage of officers, meant that good intentions were not always followed through. As a last resort, part of one of the airing yards was set aside for shot drill. This was a wholly pointless exercise whereby prisoners were issued with a 14 or 28lb shot, which they placed on the ground at their feet. On command of the warder, they crouched and raised the shot, moved one pace to their right, and returned the shot to the ground. So the exercise continued, to what little purpose we shall not know.

The vagrants were treated, or no longer treated, as a separate issue. Their numbers had increased to the point where their needs threatened to swamp the resources available to the justices, and any thoughts of their salvation were set aside. Of all those admitted to the prison, the vagrants were those most likely to be in a wretched physical condition. Poor health often resulted in their detention in prison long after their sentence expired. The old chapel was used as their infirmary. Proposals by some of the justices to improve their accommodation in the old house of correction were bitterly opposed. The betterment of their health and morals had no priority. To the magistrates their wards were deemed *sufficient under existing circumstances*. Prison neither deterred them nor improved their conduct. Returning again and again, their presence disrupted any attempt at discipline. Of the 800 prisoners committed to the gaol in 1851, most are dealt with under the Vagrancy Acts. The chaplain considered them *a class beyond redemption*.

The cost and futility of forcing so many casuals through the system, together with unfavourable observations by the prison inspectors, eventually brought change to the prisons of Lindsey. The imprisonment of vagrants now began to fall markedly. It is not clear why. Their numbers may have fallen – industry that reduced the need for labour on the land was hungry for new workers. The new county police may have been less concerned to prosecute the trampers and casuals than the old parish constables. Maybe the economics of the matter had driven a policy decision. Whatever the cause, at the end of 1853 a committee was appointed to consider the best means of separating the male prisoners at night.

Accepting their recommendations, the gaol at Spilsby was improved. Stoves were used to heat the ground floor, the cells were lit with gas, a schoolroom was erected and fitted out, and the services of a schoolmaster and mistress engaged. Henceforth female prisoners were excluded from the main building at Louth and, apart from those due to appear at court, are lodged at Spilsby. The services of the female turnkey at Louth were dispensed with, the matron had died, and the keeper's daughter, Sarah Brian, was named to take her place as and when required.

The old prison was taken out of use as a vagrant ward, and the day rooms converted to separate cells. The justices intended the men should sleep in their own room at night.

The reduction in casuals made more room for the minor offenders, the misdemeanants, passing through the prison. Locally born lads, about 200 every year, were regularly sentenced by the justices at the petty sessions or magistrates court. Half could not read or write, many had families, and few had been to prison before. They were basket and rope makers, carpenters, millers, blacksmiths and grooms, silk weavers and sawyers, potters, cotton spinners, labourers and farm servants, jugglers and showmen, surgeons and seamen, run-away apprentices, pedlars, paupers and bricklayers.

Some had deserted the militia or run away from service at sea, some were drunk and disorderly and had assaulted the constable, others hawked goods without a licence, or had taken kindling from the woods and partridge out of season, or had disobeyed their employer, and most lacked sureties to keep the peace. They were public nuisances. 'Hard labour' was their sentence - seven days to six months in the House of Correction, cleaning and brick breaking, picking oakum and chopping wood, and turning the wheel.

Having taken steps to separate the prisoners at night, the justices contemplated the silent and separate systems. Both systems required a high level of supervision to maintain silence at all times and prevent personal contact. In the separate system the prisoner's work and food were brought to their cell by the warder. There was no association with other inmates. When exercising in the yards they wore a restrictive mask. This system was tried for a while at Lincoln. The silent system was hardly more humane, but preventing communication between prisoners working together proved all but impossible. Benefits were doubtful, and the long-term effects considered cruel. Both systems had fallen from favour with the prison commissioners.

In October 1854 the justices decided the silent system was to be adopted *at all times* by the continual presence of a turnkey. Though the number of inmates was much reduced, 40 – 50 a day, there remained only three prison officers, now referred to as warders and soon to be dressed in prison uniform of a plain blue coat, dark trousers, cap and a belt. One warder was to supervise the tread wheel, one to oversee the workrooms, and one to instruct in the schoolroom. If each worked 10 hours a day, and took no days off, the order to maintain silence was impossible to enforce. Talking in the day rooms was the principal reason for more than 90 punishments administered that year.

In 1856 the Lindsey County Police are formed - 111 men in all, with a superintendent and 11 constables for the Louth petty sessions district. Mounted officers were to provide and care for their own horses. Henry Pye, the county treasurer, collected the police rate and administered the Fund to pay for the constabulary. The accounts were criticised by the justices for not being detailed enough, and a committee was appointed to consider whether a more effective mode of auditing and checking expenditure on the prisons might be possible. Local architect James Fowler's design for the police house and lock-up next to the prison was considered too costly and he was told to think again.

James Marshall was appointed governor in 1863 when John Brian resigned. Marshall had transferred from the county gaol at Warwick. His wife Harriett covered the occasional need for a matron. They and their seven children were to be the last residents in the keeper's house.

A return of the cattle plague in 1865 ravages the county's farms. Markets were closed, the movement of cattle prohibited and beasts slaughtered. A rate was levied to cover the cost of administration and the disposal of infected carcases. A new Prison Act set the justices back yet again. None of the Lindsey prisons conformed to the requirements, in particular the need to sleep prisoners in separate cells at night. Despite the overcrowding, shortly before Christmas 1868 one of the prisoners, Sainty Beverley, a young fisherman aged 18 years of age awaiting trial for stealing a sovereign, is able to take his own life. The expense of alterations and improvements necessary at Kirton and Louth made the justices think again about the construction of a single central jail.

Herbert Voule's prison report highlighted the problem. Including the old house of correction and the new prison buildings, Louth had no more than 50 separate cells. Apart from those on the ground floor, none could be warmed in winter, and all remained unlit. Ventilation is poor. The average daily number of men in custody was 53, the greatest number at any one time 81, and the year's total, 500.

From the prison inspector's report for 1868:

Persons detained in the prison:

	Adults	Juveniles	Total
7 days or less	97	13	110
8 to 14 days	74	13	87
15 days to 1 month	159	7	166
Between 1 and 2 months	50	4	54
Between 2 and 3 months	28	1	29
Between 3 and 6 months	8		8
Between 6 months and 1 year	7		7
Between 1 and 2 years	1		1
Penal servitude	3		3

Average daily number: 49   Total   465

On the day of inspection:

Employed on tread wheel	12
Employed in pumping water	2
Employed picking oakum	19
Cooking, washing, cleaning	6
Shoemaking	2
Mat making	1

Females now sent to Spilsby
Ordinary sleeping cells used for punishment
Supervision not sufficient to prevent communications
Treadmill power not applied to any useful purpose
No heating in the oakum room or the itch cell
2 prisoners moved to the asylum as insane
<u>The prison is being considered for closure.</u>

An aged and inadequate sewage system continued to cause trouble. The justices now realised that contamination of the prison's drinking water by seepage from their own privies was the cause of much sickness amongst the inmates. The water supply was failing.

Prisoners confined at Spilsby were photographed in case they need to be circulated in police records, and a hand-operated crushing machine and a grist mill were installed.

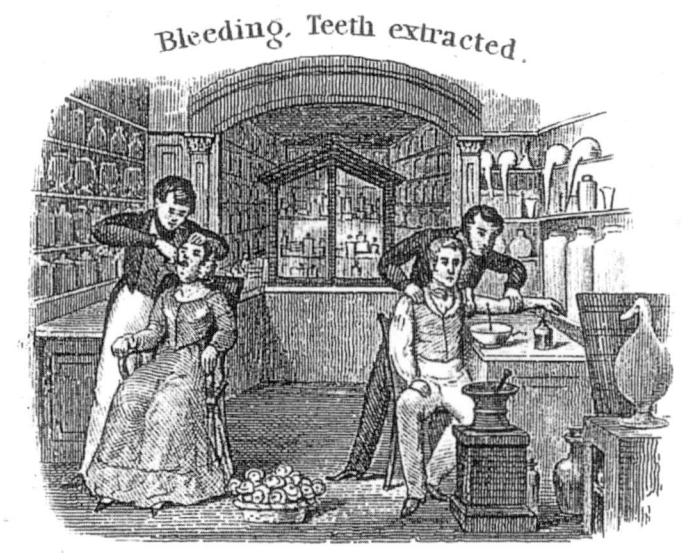

Tupholme's Chemist, Market Place, Spilsby
*Druggist and grocer. Sold candles, pickles and spices,
spring-trusses, brass enemas, soda water and lemonade.
Supplied the prison with potatoes.*
**Lindsey Quarter Sessions. A/1/650/10
Lincolnshire Archives Office**

The justices were more concerned about limiting the spread of the cattle plague than the appointment of officials to consider a new prison. Church of England ministers were appointed in every parish to oversee the movement of cattle, and there were problems over stocking of the highways with diseased animals. The payment of compensation was delayed. To allay suspicion of impropriety cattle plague accounts were to be published in county newspapers.

Almost overtaken by events, Lindsey justices were obliged to ask for an extension of time before complying with the new Prison Act. Justices at Kirton moved that a new central prison be constructed for all of Lindsey. A committee was nominated, and Grimsby, Brigg and Lincoln were considered as possible sites. 300 objections were received from landowners and ratepayers at Louth and none were in favour of the closure of the local gaol. Local justices dismissed the committee.

The magistrates at Kirton persisted with their proposal. The committee was reformed, and from January 1868 all county business was removed to special sessions sitting alternately at Grimsby and Lincoln. A decision was taken to build a central prison for the county, and by the beginning of July suitable land had been purchased in Lincoln.

The county treasurer has been in post for nearly 40 years. Born in 1799, the son of the Reverend Marmaduke Alington of Swinhope, Henry Pye had risen to a position of considerable trust in the town. His solicitor's practise, in which the son of his old headmaster, Thomas Phillips Waite, was a partner, flourished. He had changed his name to Pye under the terms of a bequest whereby he inherited an estate in Herefordshire. He coursed hounds and raced horses. He forged a number of business links in the town, and there were few local associations of which he was not a prominent member.

His ambitions outmatched his wealth. Speculative land deals were only partly successful. Substantial properties in St. Mary's Lane and Westgate, the enclosure and drainage of more than 300 acres of salt marsh at North Somercotes, and the construction of Pye's Hall drove him steadily into debt. The income of a successful solicitor's practice was unable to cover the interest on his loans.

In January his partner, Thomas Waite, was declared bankrupt. When the lands at Somercotes were put up for sale, Pye's own creditors became alarmed and it is difficult to believe local justices did not discuss his precarious solvency. Unable to cover the money he owed by the sale of estates, he faced ruin. On 17th July, Henry Pye fled from Louth.

The news devastates the town. A packed meeting of the justices, called to accept their treasurer's written resignation, heard that an audit of the accounts revealed a deficit of £5,378 in the County Fund, and a discrepancy of £4,144 in the Police Fund.

Sureties are called in. G.M. Allington and the Rev. W. Smyth responded promptly and their bonds of £2,500 each were soon deposited. Chancellor Massingberd prevaricated. He told the justices the money was available provided his legal advisors were satisfied as to his liability. Threat of legal action ensured that eventually £8,000 was recovered from the former treasurer's bonds. In future separate accounts were to be maintained for county funds, sureties for the treasurer's post were raised to £10,000, and a clerk employed to record all accounts in a ledger.

The Clerk of the Peace lays information against Pye for misappropriating and embezzling county monies and a warrant was issued for his arrest.

All hopes of retaining a jail at Louth come to an end. There will be no further expenditure on the house of correction.

In January 1872 preparations were made to remove the inmates to the new Lindsey jail in Greetham Road, Lincoln. Louth and Kirton closed on the 11th June. The service of the staff was terminated, and in October 1872 the magistrates were authorised to initiate the sale of the prison.

The days of Louth House of Correction were over.

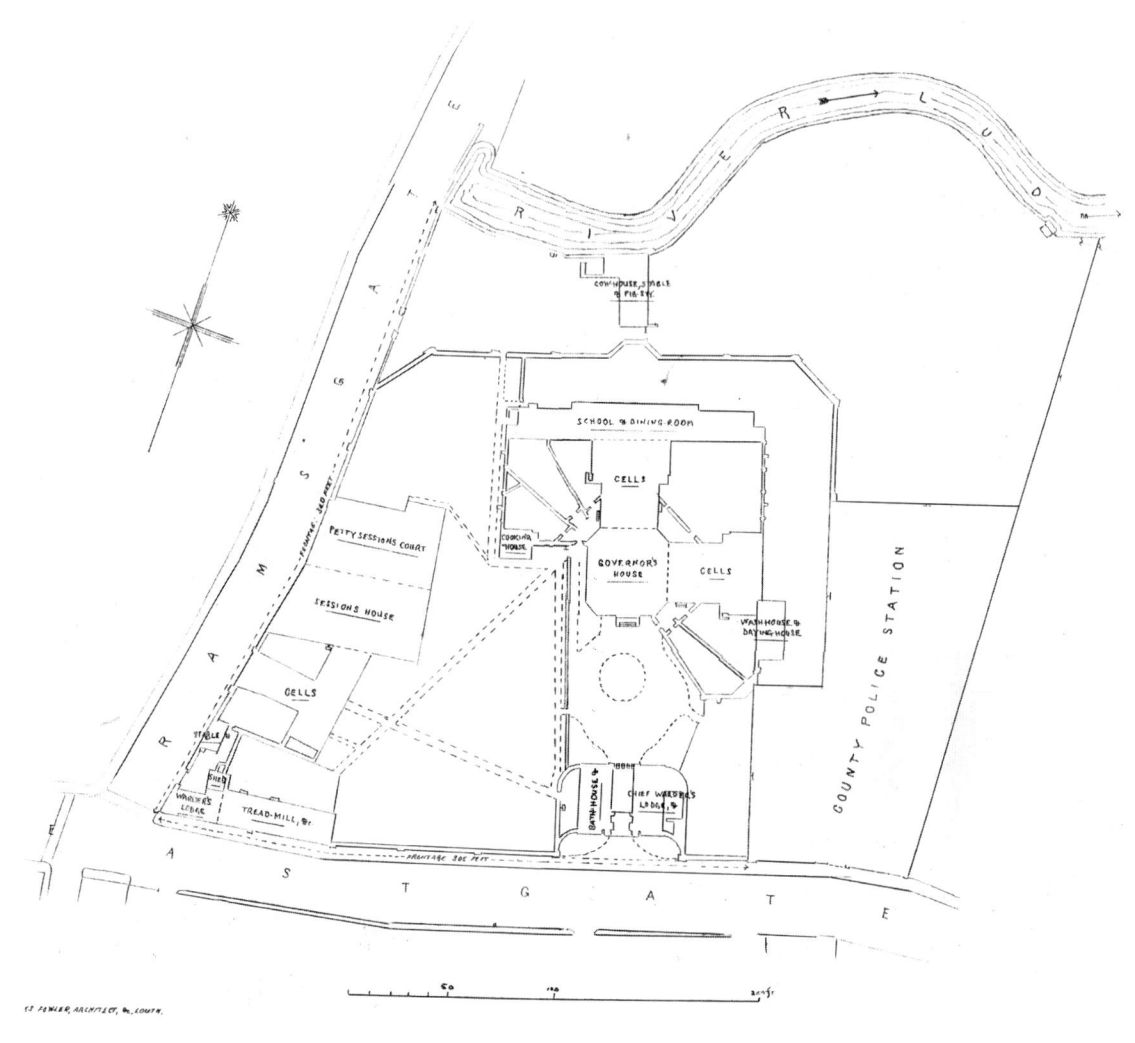

Louth Prison and grounds 1872
*James Fowler's plan was prepared for the sale of the premises.
The old House of Correction (marked on the plan as cells) and the tread wheel
sheds occupied the south west corner.*
**A.H. 1/2/4/5/2
Lincolnshire Archives Office**

- 10 -

Epilogue

TWO distinct premises served as the House of Correction in Louth. From 1827 the perimeter wall of the large Eastgate gaol encircled the dilapidated buildings of the original institution on the corner of Ramsgate.

The old house of correction was intended as a place where the idle and disorderly poor might be set to work. It reinforced the authority of Elizabethan poor law. In practise the house was increasingly used to tackle a number of social problems, not all of them compatible. Its use as a shelter for the destitute, and an infirmary for the sick and dying, compromised its role as a place of control and punishment. Houses of Correction became part of the answer to a number of social problems. With so many functions, and so few staff, success or failure was not an issue. Too many factors affecting the lives of the inmates were beyond the control of the keeper. It was enough that the House provided support for those committed to its care.

The new prison was different in construction and purpose. By the 1820s, a sentence of imprisonment, often entailing 'hard labour', was punishment in its own right. Unwisely, the justices allowed management practises that may have been appropriate to the old house of correction to be carried into the new system. Perhaps the problem of attempting to control the poor and the homeless overwhelmed them. None-the-less they failed to respond to changes in the law, or meet new requirements for places of detention. Aware of shortcomings in the old building, they accepted Kendall's design. The structure in Eastgate was wholly unsuited to its purpose. With inadequate resources and insufficient room for the prisoners, the keeper was left to manage as best he could. When the new gaol failed, the keeper took the blame.

Responsibility remained the justices'. Imprisonment, or more likely the threat of it, empowered their decisions. In the absence of a constabulary, the gaol gave the justices their authority. Whilst detention was certainly a punishment, it appears unlikely that repentance and reform were on the inmates' agenda. The prospects of many brought before the courts were so hopeless they had no fear of death, imprisonment or transportation. Their struggle to survive was enough.

Henry Pye was never brought to justice. The County Treasurer fled to Belgium where he died 15 years later at the age of 87.

Few records survived the closure of the prison. Louth museum has plans, drawn by William Foster in the 1820s, of the old house and its treadwheel. They complement those held at Lincolnshire Archives of the house in Howard's time, the specification of the new Eastgate gaol, and the drawings made on the occasion of the prison's disposal in the 1870s.

Passing mention is made of the inmates in the accounts of the Old Corporation, but more useful information is included with the Lindsey Quarter Sessions papers. They comprise three sections. Prison calendars list offenders in the gaol, their crime and often the punishment. Court minutes show the administrative role of the justices in the county, in addition to the day-to-day working of the court. Sometimes reference is made to the workings of their bridewells, gaols and houses of correction.

The session's rolls, the papers and documents produced at the sittings of the court, mainly relate to cases brought before the justices. A small number are bills produced for services and goods provided the county, and amongst these are the accounts of the keepers of the House of Correction. These accounts, especially those of the gaolers John Blythe, Thomas Waddington and Richard Cox, and the case papers, form the backbone of this story.

Reports by His Majesty's Inspectors of Prisons, so relevant to the final years, are available at the Prison Service College Library, Newbold Revel, Rugby. The college has a small museum.

The Public Record Office at Kew has a Misdemeanants Register from Louth covering the eight years from 1852 to 1859. This Register, 1,432 indexed entries, the gaol calendars and the accounts where every inmate was recorded, might prove a useful source to the family historian.

Little else remains to mark the lives of those once incarcerated within the walls of Louth House of Correction. Local merchant John Walmsley bought the grounds of the prison and the buildings at auction. When the prison was demolished, much of the material was used in the construction of 21 Victorian villas backing onto the River Lud – Walmsley Terrace. The town clock was moved to a warehouse in Queen Street, where it remains to this day. In the 1950s the cupola was dismantled and the striking bell given to St. Michael's church.

On Walmsley's death, his widow gave the vacant site to the Reverend Frederick Orme Trust. The resultant Alms houses for 11 elderly men, designed by James Fowler and built in 1885, the quiet lawns and shady trees, a sharp contrast to the airing yards and treadwheels of an earlier age.

A Prison Lay

I cannot take my walks abroad
I'm under lock and key;
And much the public I applaud
For all their care of me

Not more than others I deserve
In fact much less than more
For I have food while others starve
Or beg from door to door

The honest pauper in the street
Half naked you behold
While I am clothed from head to feet
And covered from the cold

Thousands there are who scarce can tell
Where they may lay their head
But I've a warm and well aired cell
A bath, good books and bed

While they are fed on workhouse fare
And grudged their daily food
Three times a day my meals I get
Sufficient, wholesome, good

Then to the British Public's health
Who all our cares relieves;
For while they treat us as they do
They'll never want for thieves

Anon

Louth Monthly Record and Local Advertiser   April 1869

The Orme Almshouses designed by James Fowler, and built in 1885 on the on the site of the House of Correction.

Appendix

Chaplain's Report

Spilsby House of Correction   October 10th 1844

To the Chairman of the Quarter Sessions.

Reverend Sir,
During the last year I have attended daily, in the performance of my duty, at the House of Correction at Spilsby, and now beg to lay before the Magistrates my annual Report.
This statement I make not merely because required to do so by Act of Parliament, but from an interest I hope I feel in the welfare, moral and religious, of those unfortunate beings who have been entrusted to my spiritual care.
The various apartments of the prison, with the day rooms and sleeping cells, which I frequently visit, are kept clean, orderly and well ventilated. I have been particularly gratified with the general conduct and deportment of the prisoners. Their behaviour and attention in the chapel is most exemplary and praiseworthy. As far as time and opportunity permit, I have personally inspected the juvenile offenders, and those who are willing to receive instruction, in the Church Catechism, and the principles of the Christian religion. It is not to be expected that all should become reformed characters, but there are instances where individuals have been restored from their degradations to a respectable station in society. In many cases we are labouring in vain, and hoping as it were against hope, knowing that the objects of our anxiety, upon their restoration to liberty have no alternative but to return to their former vicious habits – their being no House of Refuge – no asylum – no Penitentiary or other public establishment open for their reception, where they might be taught the means of obtaining their future livelihood. It may not be considered out of place, if I here point out a fact that comes under my own immediate observation.
A youth 18 years of age was convicted of felony at the Louth April Sessions, 1843 and sentenced to 12 months imprisonment at Spilsby. On my first interview with him, he related the following sad history of his life. That his parents were vagrants in the neighbourhood of Newcastle – that he had been brought up to vagrancy and knew nothing else. At 15 years of age his father behaved very cruelly to him, sending him out in the morning to beg and steal, and if he did not return in the evening with a sufficient quantity of plunder, beating him severely. At length being disgusted with the unnatural conduct of his father, he ran away. Has been confined for vagrancy in many different prisons, and

at last committed a Felony, for which he hoped he would have been transported. Disappointed in his expectation, he declared, that when liberated again he was determined to commit some act which would ensure a sentence of transportation, and this from necessity, not choice – being friendless, without money, and without the means of supporting himself. When he came in did not even know the letters of the Alphabet, and could merely repeat the Lord's prayer, which had been taught him by the Chaplain at Louth before his trial. Upon his expressing a wish to learn to read, we commenced in good ernest, and so successful were his endeavours that at the expiration of his imprisonment he had committed to memory the Church Catechisms with several of the Collects, could write a very decent hand, read his Bible well, and upon a slate had gone through all the useful rules of Common Arithmetic. When discharged in April last, I had the gratification to find that he was leaving the prison with views very different from those which he entertained when he came in. But what could be done? Destitute of everything, and never accustomed to work of any description, he knew not how to go about it, yet was anxious to undertake the most menial office, and to do his best, if any person could be prevailed upon to employ him. From his general good conduct, and the opinion I had formed of him, I was willing to believe there was some sincerity in his professions, which I at once determined to put to the test, and consequently took him a lodging near, employing him in the daytime on my premises on probation until May-day. During that period he conducted himself so entirely to my satisfaction, that I took the poor lad into my house as servant where he continues up to this time, well behaved, industrious, happy, and contented, and I trust I may not be disappointed in my sanguine hope that he will become by Divine grace, a redeemed character and a useful member of society.

.... The lately appointed Matron appears to be a highly respectable person, well calculated, by the necessary qualification of an even and firm temper of mind, and a kind disposition, to do credit to her appointment. I have much pleasure in reporting that she is performing the duties of her office in a very satisfactory way.

The number of prisoners committed during the year, that is to say from the 10th day of October 1843 to the 10th day of October 1844 has been 367 – viz 313 males and 54 females.

Charged with	Felony	107
	Vagrancy	81
	Poaching	17
	Misdeameanants	82
	Assault	50
	Debt	24
		367

Upon entering the prison I found

To be well educated	4
Could read and write well	19
Read and write imperfectly	164
Read only	63
Neither read nor write	117
	367

Religious Profession

Members of the Established Church	221
Roman Catholics	20
Methodists	62
Ranters	15
of Different Persuasions	14
Attend no place of worship	35
	367

Books of a moral and religious tendency are provided for the use of prisoners at the expense of the County. Many avail themselves of this privilege and are thankful for the indulgence. The books are in a very mutilated state, several years having elapsed since we had a supply. The want of waste paper I think is the chief cause of the books being torn up. I believe all possible vigilance is asked, but the delinquence cannot be detected. I wish to call the attention of the magistrates to this subject.

I have the honour to remain
Reverend Sir,
Your faithful and obedient servant,
I. Russell
Chaplain.

The Reverend Isaac Russell was the headmaster of Spilsby Grammar School, vicar at Stickford and Prison Chaplain. His report probably refers to John Nelson convicted of stealing a watch from a silversmith in Market Rasen, and sentenced to 12 months imprisonment and a whipping. Of the 34 felony prisoners appearing at court that day, five were transported to Australia for seven years or more.

Lindsey Quarter Sessions
A/1/639/51, A/2/54 and A/1/626/401/1
Lincolnshire Archives Office

LOUTH PRISON. All that is left on the site to remind the old inhabitants of the town of their Prison is the fine old pear tree in the centre of the neatly kept grounds attached to the Orme's Almshouses. It must have been very tantalizing and an additional punishment to the prisoners when taking their exercises round that tree in fruit season, their "mouths watering" the while, to see growing thereon luscious fruit of which they could not taste. Anent the diet of the prisoners, a story is told of the chaplain on one occasion visiting a well-known local character who was imprisoned. "Well C——, how are you, and how is your soul?" enquired the chaplain. "Ain't got one sir," replied the prisoner. "Tush! Tush! don't say so," exclaimed the chaplain. "How do you make that out?" "Well, sir," answered C—— "I've honly fower taters to live on, an' three on 'em 's bad 'uns, an' it wasn't enuff to keep body an' sowl togither so th' soul's flown."

Times have changed since then, and the old "House of Correction," as it was called, has given place to one of the prettiest sights in Louth, where instead of dismal prison walls, delicate tints of almond blossom meet the eye in spring, and, with the changing seasons, the ever varying tints of foliage and bloom—new and humanitarian methods for the "correction" of evil characters.

Souvenir of Louth and District c.1913

Source material and bibliography

Chapter 1   The Bridewell
Louth Poor Law assessment book 1749. Goulding 4/A/1/5
Wardens Accounts 1551-1686 LGS B/3/1
Lincolnshire Archives Office

Louth 1750 – 1860. Unpublished dissertation. J.S.N. Ogden
Lincoln Local Studies Library

Universal British Directory of Trade 1792
Grimsby Local Studies Library

A History of Louth   J.E. Swaby
Hull   1951

History, Gazeteer and Directory of Lincolnshire
William White. 1826 and 1842

Kelly's Post Office Directory of Lincolnshire 1868

British Economic and Social History 1700-1870   Philip Sauvain
Stanley Thornes 1987

Chapter 2   The Old Corporation
Louth General Sessions of the Peace minute book 1721-42.
Lindsey Quarter Sessions minute books LQS A/2/2 and A/2/3
Lindsey Quarter Sessions rolls A/1/21 and A/1/29
Muckton parish General Register 1/1
Lincolnshire Archives Office

A true and genuine confession of John Keale
Lincolnshire pamphlets   L. Lout 365
Lincoln Local Studies Library

Chapter 3   To 'a land beyond the sea'
Grand Jury Minute Book 1740-1763   COC 2/1
Lindsey Quarter Sessions minute books   LQS A/2/4-10
Lindsey Quarter Sessions rolls 1740-1763   LQS A/1/
Wardens Accounts 1735-77 LGS B/3/2
Lincolnshire Archives Office

Chapter 4   Sloth and debauchery
The State of the Prisons in England and Wales   John Howard   1784
Nottingham University Library
The Founders of Australia.
A Biographical Dictionary of the First Fleet
Mollie Gillen   Library of Australian History   Sydney 1989

Louth Old Corporation minute book 1774-1825   LGS D/1
Wardens Accounts   1777-1835   LGS B/3/3
Louth Prison. Two boxes LQS B/5
Lindsey Quarter Session minute books   1774 1787   LQS A/2/10-16
Lindsey Quarter Sessions rolls   1774-1787   LQS A/1/183-238
Lincolnshire Archives Office

Chapter 5   Against the Peace
Lindsey Quarter Sessions minute books   1787-1800   LQS A/2/16-24
Lindsey Quarter Sessions rolls   1787-1800   LQS A/1/238-294
Lincolnshire Archives Office

Chapter 6   A 'working system'
Louth prison rules 1809.   Louth Pamphlets, volume 1, Goulding Collection
Lincolnshire Local Studies Library

The State of the Prisons in England, Scotland and Wales   1812
James Neild
Prison Service College Library, Newbold Revell, Rugby

Lindsey Quarter Sessions minute books 1800-1815   LQS A/2/24-32
Lindsey Quarter Sessions rolls 1800-1815   LQS A/1/294-413
Lincolnshire Archives Office

Chapter 7   Hard Labour
Lindsey Quarter Sessions minute books 1815-1821   LQS A/2/32-36
Lindsey Quarter Sessions rolls 1815-1821   LQS A/1/294-413
Report of the Society for the Improvement of Prison Discipline 1822
Lincolnshire Archives Office

Chapter 8   New Eastgate jail – old problems
Lindsey Quarter Sessions minute books 1822-1837   LQS A/2/36-49
Lindsey Quarter Sessions rolls 1822-1837   LQS A/1/462-583
Gaol Act reports to the Secretary of State for 1823, 1824 and 1826
County Committee 7/2, 7/3 and 7/4
7th Report of the Society for the Improvement of Prison Discipline 1827
8th Report of the Society for the Improvement of Prison Discipline 1832
Louth Prison   Two boxes LQS B/5
First report of the Select Committee of the House of Lords - The Present State of the several Gaols and Houses of Correction 1835
First Report of the Commissioners on Municipal Corporations 1835. Eastern and North Western Circuits
Lincolnshire Archive Office

Chapter 9   Beyond redemption
Lindsey Quarter Session minute books   1838-1872   LQS A/2/49-74
Lindsey Quarter Session rolls   1838-1843   LQS A/1/584-631
Lincolnshire Archives Office

Annual reports of His Majesty's Inspector of Prisons   1838-1872
Prison College Library, Newbold Revell and Lincolnshire Archives Office

Misdemeanants Register for Louth Prison   May 1852 - December 1859
PCOM 2/342
Lindsey Sessions Calendars 1831-1871   PCOM 2/311 and 2/439
Public Records Office, Kew
(Some also available at Lincoln Archives Office separately and in Sessions rolls)

Louth Census returns for 1841, 1851, 1861 and 1871
HO 107/639 F32, HO 107/2111 F412, RG 9/2380 F111 and RG 10/2380 F111
The Story of Claribel   (for notes on Henry Pye)   Phyllis Smith and Margaret Godsmark   Lincoln 1965
Louth Local Studies Library

Additional reading:

Prisons for the Poor - English Bridewells 1555-1800   Joanna Innes
Labour, Law and Crime   Francis Smyder and Douglas Hay
Tavistock 1987

Victorian Prison Lives   An English Prison Biography 1830-1914
Philip Priestly   Methuen 1985

Oxford History of the Prison   Norval Morris and David Rothman
Oxford University Press   1995

Rural Crime in the Eighteenth Century   B.J. Davey
University of Hull Press   1994

English Local Government Vol 6 English Prisons under Local Government
Sidney and Beatrice Webb   Frank Cass and Co   1963

The Fatal Shore.   A History of the Transportation of Convicts to Australia 1787-1868
Robert Hughes   Pan Books   1988

Index

Accounts	10 24 42 50 72 78 101 113
Alford	7 41
Almshouses	7 116 118
Assaults	22 51 55 97
Bailiff	27 46
Barton on Humber	15 44
Bastardy	15 46 60 64
Births	58
Black Assize	30
Bolton, Rebecca	36
Brackenbury, Joseph	72 87
Breach of the Peace	22 49
Bridewell	8 11 30 34 35 40 51 59 63
Caistor	40
Calendar	28 64 73 88
Capital offences	10 20 87
Carpet manufactory	96
Cattle plague	112
Chapel	60 85
Chaplain	31 34 52 58 85 93 99-100 108 119-121
Civil unrest	63 77 87
Clock tower	14 60
Common gaols	11 30 34 35
Confession	17
Conscription	16 19 31 50 63
Constables	13 16 24 27 46 49 87 99
Convict hulks	38 98
Coroner	58 74
Corporation	8 9 10 13 21 22 89
County Assize	20 30
County police	110
County gaols	64
Coupland, Eleanor	40-41
Deaths	38 58 73 86 94 97 103 110

Debtors	18 30 32 51 58 60
Destitute poor	8 22 44 50 52 58 63 65 73
Dietary	18 27 35 59 85 90 101 103
Dissenters	14 46
Education	86 100 108
Edward VI's charter	9
Employment	18 40 52 54 59 66 100 108
Escapes	13 21 45 53 55 104
Examination	48
Fairs	51 104
Female prisoners	53 70 75 89 95
Fire	15 49 52
Firearms	57
First Fleet	38
Fittings	42 52 53 56 57 70 79
Folkingham	35
Gainsborough	11 21 34 36 39 40
Gibbet irons	20
Grand Jury	7 16 17 41 46 47
Grantham	59
Greetham	7 112
Hard labour	105 109
Hemp	18
Highways	14 26 46
Horncastle	14 54 55
Howard, John	29-32 66 79
Inventory	82
Johnson, John	94 98
Jury	9 13 16 23 46 47
Justices	9 13 14 16 22 26 30 39 46 54 73 93 99 112

126

Keale, John	19	Rules	42 67 89 101
Keeper	18 21 24 27 32 39 51 55 70 87 92 93 95 110	Segregation	8 27 31 36 40 53 56 60 64 77 105 109
Keeper's lodging	53 83	Separate system	109 110
Kendall, Henry Edward	77 83	Sessions Hall	13 45 46 54 60
Kirton	40 51 59 63 64 94 110	Settlement	15 47 23
		Short, Mary	48
Lincoln Castle	11 17 18 20 24 35 39 59	Shot drill	108
Lindsey	7 10 11 44 54 72	Silent system	109 110
Louth Navigation	24 26	Smallpox	45
Lunacy	30 40 54	Spalding	35
Lying in	44 58	Spilsby	19 77 78 79 82 86 109 111 119
		Spirituous liquor	35 39
Matron	56 59 70 87 91 109 110	Spittal	16
Medical care	17 32 33 34 43 44 57 58 72 86 94 97	Stamford	35 59
		Stonebow Gate	34
Militia	47 51	Stotherd, John	54-55 65
Mill	68 70 85 90	Supplies	72
Misdemeanants	16 56 60 73 84 87 109 116	Surgeon	31 32 44 58 86 90 101
Muckton	119	Town plan	12
		Transportation	18 23 24 27 37 36 37 49 50 98
Padley, J.S.	80 105	Treadmill	62 68-72 75 85 90 94 101 108
Penitentiaries	66	Tumbril	20
Petty sessions	9 16 37 73 74 75 101	Turnkey	60 64 68 87 94 95 101 110
Petty sessions court	101 106	Turnpike	24 26
Poor Law	8 17 44 65	Typhus	30
Prison inspectors	89 90 93 94 101 103 105 111 116		
Prison plan	25 75 114	Uniform	59 83
Prison wing	80 81		
Provisions	9 57 72 101 102 112	Vagrants	4 22 44 57 65 73 83 93 99 103 108 109
Punishment	9 13 59 87 94 95 110	Visiting committee	24 27 32 34 36 40 52 95
Punishment cells	51 59 94		
Pye, Henry	87 105 110 113	Visitors	58 86
Quarter sessions	9 11 16 23 36 41 46-50 54 64	Warden	9 11 16 46
Quarter sessions court	105 106 107	Whipping	10 13 22 41 44 48 66 97
		Workhouse	95 99
Rats	45		
Reception	57 83 97		
Reform	8 29-32 66 79 89 100		